I Fought the Law and . . . I Won!

By Johnny Cordero

A man fights for his little boy, lost in the shadows of Eastern Europe

DEDICATION

To the tired, to the poor ... to the huddled masses yearning to breathe free.; to those innocent people unjustly ruined, destroyed and driven to insanity.

*Excerpt from the Statute of Liberty

ACKNOWLEDMENTS

Cover Design © 2017 by John Michael Cordero

Cover Art by DesignChest

Cover Picture by Shutterstock, used by permission

Worth Wren Jr., a writer/journalist/consultant who reviewed, proofread and edited this work.

Special thanks to the many individuals quoted in the "Hall of Shame" chapter. They graciously and voluntarily contributed their stories.

Dr. Palmira Ubinas, a gifted writer who provided guidance in making this book possible.

Dr. Gilbert Marez, a true mentor, founder and minister of the Camino De Paz Church of Fort Worth, Texas, who made it possible for me to work on this book; most of it was written in a lonely room in the church's alternate classroom.

My son Johnny, Jr. who gave me permission to put our story in a book.

Angela Acevedo, my mother and first teacher.

My Dreams Academy

1516 N Sylvania Ave
Fort Worth, TX 76111
(972) 876-9861
www.Foughtthelawandwon.com
Or email: IFoughtandWon@yahoo.com

DISCLAIMER by the author:
This book contains the opinions and ideas of its author. Relevant laws vary from state to state. Strategies outlined in this book may not be suitable for every individual and are not guaranteed or warranted to produce any particular results.

Although the author and publisher made every effort to ensure that the information in this book was correct at press time, the author and publisher do not assume and hereby disclaim any liability to any party for any loss or risk, damage or disruption, personal or otherwise, which is incurred as a consequence, directly or indirectly, caused by errors or omissions whether such errors or omissions result from negligence, accident, of the use and application of any of the contents of this book.

I am not issuing legal advice through this book; that's not the intent. For legal advice, the reader should consult a competent attorney in the pertinent legal field. The reader is advised to check with a legal professional or other specialist before taking any steps outlined in this book. What is written here is my own personal experience and findings in my own particular case. Actual names and places, in most instances cited herein, are omitted to protect privacy and the innocent. It has been my purpose to provide you with an enlightening, practical tool in case you walk in my shoes.
Johnny Cordero

Book web site: www.Foughtthelawandwon.com

ISBN: 978-0-578-19731-9

Library of Congress Control Number: 2017914069
Law and Literature

MY DREAMS
ACADEMY

www.mydreamsacademy.org

TABLE OF CONTENTS

Pay heed to these REAL cases:

An 18-year-old man was ordered to pay child-
support for a 13-year-old;
never mind that the "father" was 5 when the
child was born!

*

Despite two DNA paternity tests confirming he
was not the father,
a man was jailed for failure to pay support for
the child!

*

A man was ordered to pay $30,000 in
retroactive support for a child not his!

*

An exemplary American father escapes after being
held hostage for more than three months during
the Iraq war· Upon returning to the United
States, he's jailed for being $1,425 in arrears on
child-support·

1

FOREWORD

Making an 'impossible dream' a reality

Like the plot of a Hollywood movie, this book conveys drama, suspense and the love of a father in search of solutions to find and parent his little boy who at first lived hidden in the shadows of Eastern Europe.

This legal and parenting battle began outside the jurisdiction of the United States and then moved to Texas. Johnny Cordero engaged in a legal battle against a system that threatened injustice in a case of child custody and access.

This story touched my heart because, contrary to most imprudent parents in a similar situation, Johnny showed throughout his legal fight his filial love and his dedication to parental and financial responsibilities. And fought without regards to economic and personal sacrifice to gain access to his son.

It was a long, tedious, nerve-jangling and frustrating process since there was little legal protection of his parental rights, there were no guarantees that he would be able to nurture his child and there was even the chance that he would never see the boy again.

This father moved heaven and earth to find traces of his former lover and their child. He explored filing an international legal case in a strange country. He learned the pertinent laws first and researched his case before beginning the legal process.

Johnny ran the gamut of feelings, from helpless and hopeless to jubilant. Too often misled or misinformed by greedy or inept lawyers, he suspected the family law system of corruption, bias against fathers and/or failing to hold the child's wellbeing as top priority.

My admiration for Johnny is genuine. He climbed a craggy, often seemingly insurmountable mountain. He never gave up on giving his beloved son the best long-distance family possible spanning thousands of miles.

What would have seemed impossible for many became a personal challenge to this courageous man who put on hold his personal dreams and career in the face of possible emotional and financial ruin.

His journey gave him new strength and his life, new meaning.

I Fought The Law and I Won can serve as an inspiration to the regular guy afflicted with a similar legal situation. Johnny's book is more than just a personal story.

It's a reliable document that can guide thousands who find themselves walking in Johnny's shoes.

Congratulations to Johnny Cordero for this extraordinary legacy that, through his astonishing research and experience, has left the world a potentially better place. The book is more than a guide through a legal maze. It shows that the unconditional love of a father can realize the "impossible dream."

I Fought The Law and I Won might set a precedent in the history of this nation.

Dr. Palmira Ubinas
Poet, Author
President, International Association of Hispanic Writers, Art and Culture
Cultural Ambassador, ArtePax, Spain
Universal Ambassador of Peace-Switzerland; Paris, France
President, II World Congress of Writers
Doctor Honoris Causa, Latin-American Academy of Literature

INTRODUCTION – *My legal trek began with a kiss.*

I fathered a child, without being married! A decision I made totally against my principles and values.

Like mine, our society has many child-custody and support tales defying logic, common sense, fairness – many of them beginning with a kiss and ending with a lawsuit. At the start, the scariest unknown was where my legal battle would be fought; the woman whom I once loved lived in Eastern Europe.

Yes, a kiss sparked my own adventure into parenthood, but my family law journey began with a little boy, at the time still an embryo in his mother's womb. Because of the boy, I took on *a 900-pound gorilla* -- the twisting and turning legal possibilities of the family courts-- and I prevailed! Well, it was a victory but not one to gloat over.

As I wrote this book, I thought of the lad, my son, but also of you the reader. My heart goes out to those good people whose lives have been ruined confronting a very powerful legal system of which they knew nothing, but under whose mercy they pleaded.

For me, as the legendary writer Charles Dickens' novel states:

"It was the best of times; it was the worst of times!"

I fathered a child, went through a horrendous legal fight for the right to be with my son. I lost, prevailed, won again, and finally succeeded in a rare moment for a mother-leaning state.

My boy was lost in the shadows of Eastern Europe.

I fathered a child, what a despicable act! I fathered a child out of wedlock. What a despicable crime! I was not proud of my achievement at first. Another kind of "despicable me," and this was far from the animation of Hollywood.

So, I decided to write about the unusual experiences I had in family court, hoping to give fathers in similar situations a passionate guide to realizing their dreams and hopes of fatherhood. This book can save you lots of headaches and money, and the endless aches that come from making disastrous legal mistakes. To my knowledge, this is the first and only book on the market written on the subject by someone other than a family lawyer.

Most available books on the subject are written in very general terms and intended to entice the reader to hire the lawyer who wrote it. My book, to the contrary, serves as a practical guide and helpful tool.

I often wish that realities could mirror fiction. If only we could create the plot, the happily-ever-after ending . . .

The story is told of two identical twin brothers walking along a road, seeking help in the middle of a blizzard one night, eventually seeing a modern farmhouse with fireplace, swimming pool and expensive landscaping. They approached, knocked on the door; it cracked open.

A lovely young woman peeked out, with door chain in place.

"We're stranded; our vehicle broke down," one twin said. "We wonder if you could put us up for the night. In the morning we can work on our car."

The lady said she had just been widowed and lived alone. "I have a barn out back where you can spend the night, but you must not come into the house."

Grateful, the bachelor brothers trudged to the barn, spent the night. Early next day, they repaired their SUV and drove away.

A year later, after a series of unpublicized family court hearings and decisions on a mostly uncontested paternity suit, Jim visited his twin, who lived in a distant county.

"Thomas, do you remember the widowed lady who allowed us to sleep in her barn last year?" Thomas said he did.

"While I was asleep in the barn," Jim asked, "did you sneak into her house in the middle of the night and have sex with her?"

"Well, yes," Thomas said· "I won't deny it· **Her kisses were sweeter than wine**· But why do you ask?"

Jim reported that he had just gone through some family court hearings; Thomas expressed surprise, then became suspicious·

"And when you snuck in," Jim said, "did you tell the lady that your name was James Smith, not Thomas, giving her my name?"

"Listen, first let me apologize to you· That wasn't right, I have to admit," Thomas insisted, sounding truly sorry· "What happened?"

"No problem, Thomas· In fact, I'm grateful for your deception, my brother· You see, the lady named me – James Smith – as the father of her now 3-month-old son· Jane said I *fathered the child, and soon I agreed· Now*

we're married and I am co-owner of the farm,

the plush homestead and her substantial

investments and savings!"

Another "if only": If only every paternity case ended so happily . . .so comfortably and with humor . . . !

If you, the reader, are seeking a way out of supporting what I call **fathering** your children, my book is **<u>NOT</u>** for you. Put it down and walk away. May life return to you ten-fold everything you wish for your child!

In this book, I aim to help, to inspire, to educate, to give hope to all parents who remain – like I was – ignorant of the nooks, the crannies, uncertainties, surprises, the strange reasoning and the complexities of family court. Perhaps the fathers needing my help most, I thought, would be those who often must leave their home state to make a living and those who don't have the monetary power or zeal to fight in court. Think: busy truck drivers, laborers, construction workers, the hard-working fathers-to-be, the young parent, fathers whose jobs often send them away for long periods of time, men having done wrong but wanting to do right, men wronged by a powerful system. These men rarely have the time, drive and the energy to do what I did.

For you I stood in the arena of legal gladiators…

I only had but a few stones in my bag and there was a Goliath, a giant legal system.

I fought your fight and won it!

I owe you this book!

Chapter 1 – *The 27-second phone chat with a receptionist was billed at $94.*

It was the year 2009. . . . I was on the phone with my attorney's receptionist for less than a minute, exactly 27 seconds, to confirm my family court hearing scheduled the following day in Dallas. Three days later I received my attorney's invoice billing me $94 for that call, or at the rate of $12,533 per hour!

Indeed, probably the world's most expensive attorney, who had previously advertised a fee rate of $250 an hour! Realities can be surprising.

It was only the latest of too many dubious episodes. A five-year, pitfall-plagued, emotion-riddled, international legal quest to be the good American father that I craved, hungered to be, dreamed nightly of being – for my European son. The woman I once found alluring tried to bargain for more child-support money. At stake for me, at risk for me, was the major personal role I wanted to play in my child's life! To play that role, I had to come up with money I did not have and could not possibly afford to give.

Ironically, she thought she was aiming for the best outcome for our son. To be fair about her motives, I have to admit she was gambling on winning a bigger pot of financial security for our son and herself.

Meanwhile, I was losing faith in both the honor and professionalism of our legal system, particularly among our lawyers. Some of my attorneys did win some battles for me, but also took financial advantage of me while I was emotionally vulnerable.

*****

My Judgment:

Be aware that some lawyers will save you money on court proceedings or perhaps win for you what appears to be a bountiful settlement, but then charge you for something previously unexpected.

In the end, your windfall savings or award can be relocated to your attorney's pocketbook!

*****

Here's an example:

A Dallas attorney took the case of a Hispanic woman crippled in a Texas traffic mishap. The victim had emerged from her car after stopping with a flat tire. While awaiting help, she was struck by a passing vehicle and injured severely.

After nearly two years of medical care and rehabilitation efforts, she was awarded $72,000 when her lawsuit was settled.

To her amazement, she pocketed only $7,200 – 10%. Her attorney kept the rest.

In fairness, the attorney deserves some credit for paying for his client's extended stay in a hotel, with meals included, because she could not work. Maybe the idea of the victim staying with relatives never worked. Whatever, a sizeable portion of her settlement went to pay for her two-year hotel stay. As it turns out, the lawyer negotiated and paid a reduced rate with the cheapest hotel in town, then charged the woman at the rate of a five-star hotel and pocketed the difference!

I know the woman. She still suffers from effects of the injuries and the settlement's limited help, her $7,200 now long gone along with her dream of a better life in America.

*****

My Judgment:
To be fair about possible extenuating circumstances, consider that the lawyer

might be saddled with his/her law school/student loan debt, a family vacation, that sports car ... the kids' tuition.

And who mandated professionalism? Are lawyers there to serve anyone with selfless dedication?

I have to say I believe that most lawyers are hard-working, sincere and honest professionals – a good number are dear friends, honorable people. I'm not knocking the whole legal profession, but there are some bad apples in the barrel; some doctors also are scoundrels, and so are a number of mechanics, insurance agents and real estate brokers. And don't get me started on that insurance agent, highly recommended by a friend, that agent who promised me big savings and later quoted me a rate at twice what I was paying!

Million-dollar smiles apparently come with the territory.

There are crooks everywhere, it seems, and there are lawyers who make a mockery of their so-called legal profession; they sometimes prey on the vulnerable clients!

*****

In 1997, a man named Sammy Sorrell offered broader, decidedly more negative and controversial views of the legal profession, as reflected in his controversial book, _Lawyers Destroying America._ Here's a summary of a few of his claims:

> "_More than 100,000 formal complaints are filed annually against U.S. lawyers and lawyer-judges, but only 2 percent are ever formally prosecuted._" Sorrell accuses attorneys of robbing their clients via over-billing and outright theft, conspiracy and fraud.

Sorrell was a writer based in Albuquerque, N.M., national director for United States Citizens for Legal Reform and a talk show host.

These accusations are a bit scary in a nation where legal reforms have been undertaken but many more are still advocated and awaiting government action.

I attended college with a fellow who became a lawyer. One day he told me that I ought to consider becoming a lawyer as there is good money to be made. He went further and said that he charged clients whatever he wanted and, surprisingly, they paid it. He would receive settlements for his clients and kept the money for himself! At times he was not showing up for court to represent clients, especially when they ended up with unfavorable judgments against them. I guess he went on too long and things caught up with him because, not long after, he was disbarred and imprisoned. Last I heard, he was a repairman for a swimming pool company.

Shady practices have led many lawyers to disbarment – i.e., having their license to work as a lawyer revoked. Once disbarred, a career in law is most likely ended although, in rare moments, a new license to practice may be issued by another state.

Perhaps you've heard of the controversial, brilliant and legendary F. Lee Bailey, the lawyer who was on the legal team defending legendary football player O.J. Simpson in the notorious murder case that was later dubbed the "trial of the century." Among Bailey's other clientele were Patty Hearst, the billionaire newspaper empire heiress charged with armed robbery crimes after being kidnapped by radical Symbionese Liberation Army criminals/extremists of the 1970s; Dr. Sam Sheppard, who was accused of murdering his wife and became the source subject of "The Fugitive" TV series and movie; and Albert DeSalvo, the infamously sadistic Boston Strangler.

Though a brilliant defense lawyer, Bailey was disbarred in Florida in 2001, for failure to turn in funds forfeited by a drug-smuggling client as part of a court agreement. For some, earning a few million dollars a year is still not enough-----indeed, love of money is the root of all evils. In 2003, Massachusetts followed suit, disbarring Bailey for similar reasons. Even after he passed the Maine bar exam, Bailey's 2012 application to practice law in that state weaved through litigation for two years. He was denied a license in 2014. As of this writing, after his appeals failed, Bailey remains disbarred. He however went on and completed a master's degree in business administration and serves as a consultant for large companies. The mark stays on his record. Probably still a legend, but a tainted legend at best. A 2017 report states that he has filed for bankruptcy.

How on earth one of the world's best criminal lawyers ended like that?

More recently, a very successful and popular lawyer from Dallas was disbarred and imprisoned for theft, fraud and for keeping settlement funds for himself and returning none to his clients. He would also take on loans using his clients' funds as collateral.

Regardless of how bright, rich or famous the lawyer may be, the legal profession aims to hold lawyers to the highest standards of ethics and has tools to keep them honest. It has little tolerance for crooks!

I cannot blame the legal profession for any of my troubles, but I encountered some lawyers whom I will never recommend or trust again. For a portion of my challenges and regrets, I can blame the shysters sometimes found in the profession.

Until a better world comes along, we have to live with reality. The reality is – in the practice of law, mechanics, medicine, insurance, education, even the religious ministries and our societal sector in general – there are blood-sucking sharks or vampires ready to prey on the less fortunate and devour the naïve clientele.

In May 2017, I received very sad news about an acquaintance. This individual was a very successful, respected businessman. He had moved to the United States with a wife and a child and little money. In just seven years, however, he started a business and accumulated more than 15 million dollars! That's what the published stories reported. His story was so worth telling that he was featured in newspapers and television, and he spoke at conferences and even became president of the local Chamber of Commerce. Pictures flashed all over with him driving in a Roll-Royce and riding a Hartley-Davidson motorcycle…and wearing thousand-dollar suits, Armani shirts, silk ties and a million-dollar smile. He was the man of the hour, gifted, charismatic, a true example to emulate! The real "American Dream," the Golden Boy.

But all of this was just so much hype, an illusion that too many people came to believe.

There, on Facebook, I saw this man's arrest profile picture, posted by investors, people claiming to have been scammed by this acquaintance. Apparently, his charisma alone convinced many suckers to believe in riches, quick bucks, to be made, just as he reportedly had done. His touted success in business convinced many to invest in his company. People poured in by the thousands to invest in his business; a dear friend invested, and lost, nearly $200,000!

Reports indicate it was all, or nearly all, a scam. He was not licensed as an investment broker, and most of his claims were dubious. Further, he was here undocumented and, to top it all off, was involved in money laundering – the investigators claimed – for drug cartels. There was his picture, the success story … the entrepreneur, the American dream. The criminal charges ranged from fraud to theft, to money laundering and immigration violation.

The lessons one must learn from all of this: don't envy, get rid of greed, walk through life at your own pace, not someone else's; don't keep up with the Joneses, don't covet. For if you do, you will dig your own grave. Further, if a business proposal sounds too good to be true, it probably is. I always walk away from anyone who offers a quick return on investment; if they insist, I then ask that they show me their bank statement posting the money they claim to make. Thus far, no one has done so!

I learned my lessons during my high school years. In those energetic, hormone-driven days I was introduced to a very appealing multilevel business. An acquaintance said, "Don't worry, we don't sell vitamins, we don't sell soap either." The offer was that, by working part-time I would draw full-time money. That sounded pretty good to me. I was invited to a house owned by a top leader, an eight-bedroom castle, six-car garage, heated swimming pool, Jacuzzi, home theatre and many more luxuries. I jumped on the wealth wagon immediately, signed up and went to work long hours to try to make even more money. The promise of part-time hours soon disappeared as I often found myself talking to someone until late hours of the night and weekends. I slept, breathed, dined and sold my soul for this business. I pestered everyone coming my way and made them feel guilty and foolish for not joining the business of the rich and famous like me (I drove a 23-year old car with more than 260,000 miles on the odometer, to meet my clients daily and slept on my Mom's couch).

I spoke as if I were already there, at the top of the pyramid. Yes, I was full of it.

After several years of hard work and a few lost friends, I had no commendable money. I still slept on my mother's couch, drove the old Pinto and wore the same clothes. No money in the bank either. All that in spite of bringing in good money.

You see, there is a side that's never told. As I moved up the ladder bringing in good money, I was expected to spend that money on plane tickets to attend conferences, cover travel expenses and fancy hotels, membership fees, enrichment books. Most of the money went to paying the people whom I brought in and also attending seminars to hear someone tell how they got very rich in the same business. The organization I managed brought in $3,700 a month; not bad for a high school kid working "part-time", in the 80's.

People came to me, in awe of my supposed success, asking for advice ..., but I had no money!

The alleged "facts" began to unravel as I found out how the leader's wealth came about. The castle mansion where the leader lived, the guy said to be at the top of the chain, turned out to be inherited. He also was a well-compensated retired engineer and his wife, a psychologist with a Ph.D. and a hefty salary and benefits. Additionally, they had inherited substantial amounts of money and other properties. Nothing of the purported wealth that I saw came from the multilevel enterprise. Like me, they were just starting.

I realized I had jumped on a boat that had a hole in it and would soon sink.

After putting in several years of honest effort, I quit…with nothing to show for all my work, time, lost friends and other sacrifices.

The lesson is that old one: If a business sounds too good to be true, it probably is. *That was my first time being taken!*

My point is, lawyers are not the only ones to blame. There are blood-sucking sharks and vampires everywhere, ready to prey on the less fortunate and devour the naïve clientele.

Now let's get back to discussing my case….

On my family law adventure, at first, I was optimistic about my chances in court. My outlook would soon turn to pessimism.

My Latino roots – with distinctly brown skin, dark eyes and black though prematurely graying hair – and the ethnic, semi-racial bias fairly common in this part of the world should have already taught me to distrust the white culture at all levels as I tried to give my fair-haired, clear-eyed infant all the love, attention, support, learning and security that could possibly come from a father living some 6,000 miles away. In my world I had already dubbed him *Johnny Jr.*

My reality: To become the jet-hopping father that I wanted to be would cost me more than $18,000 in legal fees and another $12,000 trying to gain shared custody. And I knew that custody was likely a pipedream, likely the impossible dream.

If anything similar to mine, your legal fight will be costly.

I write to suggest, recommend, ways to save you money, headaches and time.

But this book is not legal advice, as I am not a family lawyer. For any specific legal advice on custody, child-support or such, you are advised to seek legal counsel from a competent family lawyer. I would share however that, like other career professionals, lawyers become specialists in different legal fields. For litigation in family court, I recommend, engage the services of a competent family law specialist with a good attorney reputation. Check with friends and acquaintances; ask for references, and check them out. As simple and basic as this advice sounds, I warn you to be extra cautious in the screening process.

In my case, because of the many challenges, I consulted with two lawyers in Europe and another nine American lawyers, six of which represented themselves as family specialists. I consulted with a recent graduate of law school, among the nine, and then there was a young general practice lawyer who was recommended by an old semi-retired family lawyer because of some familiarity with international cases. I further consulted with another generalist who danced circles around my questions. The others included a former district attorney who gave me ill advice, a family lawyer with 30-plus years in the field, a family law specialist with her own practice, an appeals lawyer, a very bright/top-dollar lawyer, and – I believe – the best appellate attorney lawyer in the U.S. Southwest.

In the beginning, though, I represented myself; I was a defendant and my own attorney, self-represented – attorney *pro se,* effectively – while dealing with several lawyers in Europe and in the United States.

In the United States you do have the right to represent yourself in court, although you might be going against a family law specialist, a hard-nosed courtroom heavyweight, a legal eagle equal to Mike Tyson, and you might get knocked out in the very first round and land on your behind!

If you decide to represent yourself, you've got to elude embarrassments by learning court procedures and rules, documenting everything in writing, learning how to talk to the opposite counsel and the judge, and thereby, mastering the jargon to address the court. You must learn how to cross-examine witnesses. My self-representation led the opposing lawyers to work through and with me and to share with me the documents, transcripts, copies of everything they had, the scope of their legal reasoning and ideas about strategy…12,000 pages of good ammunition for my own defense!

It was a fight for my honor, a fight for my own survival as a self-respecting father, a fight for my lasting peace and my future. I would face a colossal system with unlimited resources that potentially could drive me to ruin – a formidable army with the best weapons.

I was, in turn, a regular guy, a midget in a land of giants!

My first move was to randomly select a European law firm via Google; we corresponded by emails, and I bombarded the firm's partners with questions.

I phoned them from the States and spent time picking their minds; it was both, expensive and time-consuming and often lacking fruit. I then flew to Europe to meet with two of the bunch. I presented my research results and explained the way I wanted my case to proceed against the plaintiff, my former lover, in a European court.

But months went by with no action, and payments to the two lawyers bought little sympathy. They spoke as if Donald Trump stood with an open box of cash in front of them. We wined and dined, but at my expense, and they spoke of assembling a winning legal team; they called it "a dream team." They appeared to have in mind something like the O.J. Simpson defense team of star litigators, including a version of F. Lee Bailey. On my budget, that idea was a silly joke. We talked of strategies and possible trial fees, but I just could not come to trust them or their courts. We never went to court there. If I had stuck with

27

them, I believe I would still be fighting court battles there today, all the way to the next century.

So, I returned to the United States and continued corresponding with the lawyers via email. I gained a wealth of legal knowledge plus understanding of the differences between international and U.S. legal systems. I was preparing for trial.

My major victory in Europe, though, was a holding pattern. I kept the case from going international, particularly to The Hague. Although there are international treaties and international family crimes to deal with, the international courts will respect the jurisdiction of in-country courts in most legal family matters and will not try to force its authority on the national and local courts of the world. I believe I would have lost by fighting in international courts.

I discovered that I had to win my legal battles on the home courts.

Still, first, there was an expansive wealth of legal information to cover before I discovered my path. I invested well over 5,000 hours learning….. *Better get an attorney!*

Again, lawyers specialize.

My recommendation: DO NOT – *PLEASE!* – do not choose a lawyer for a family law case just because he/she is a family friend. Do not choose a lawyer just because he/she won a case for you on a car accident. Rather, secure the services of a lawyer who has proven competency, a successful track record, in family law. Makes obvious sense doesn't it. If you don't, you will likely waste your money on a losing cause. On this family case, the good neighborhood lawyer would not work!

To illustrate my point, I use a significant case that won worldwide attention. You may recall the case of President Bill Clinton having an affair with a White House intern named Monica Lewinsky. A special prosecutor was chosen to find the facts as to whether the president had violated any law. The special prosecutor subpoenaed Ms. Lewinsky to testify and provide information, but she refused and hired a lawyer who had represented her family successfully in a variety of lawsuits. As a physician, her father had faced some allegations of malpractice, but was successfully defended by attorney William H. Ginsburg.

In the end, Ms. Lewinsky had to fire Ginsburg and hire lawyers knowledgeable on this type of case. As a litigator friend shared, "this lawyer was not the right lawyer to face the special prosecutor."

I spent lots of money on my legal quest, but my time was worth a lot more; as I mentioned, I worked more than 5,000 hours on my case. I would have made hundreds of times more money than my lawyers had I been paid for the hours that I personally spent in court and on researching and reading laws, explanations of laws, cases and court decisions and other legal documents, on meetings with lawyers, corresponding with lawyers . . . and doing other related legal homework and legwork. Most hard-working parents do not have the time, zeal and energy to do what I did.

I spent nights, afternoons, weekends and holidays on my quest. I spent time in libraries and bookstores, on the Internet and on the phone. I talked with lawyers, friends, anyone who could contribute. Herein, in this book, I share the wealth I gathered from my research.

But I needed to do it. I had to do it. I had to be a father to my son. MY SON, lost in the shadows of Eastern Europe! If you have a child and that child is not in your household, not yours to hold and listen to, not yours to play games with, not yours to go camping with, not yours to share your life with, … every day, anytime, … then do what I did: *Stop sobbing, stop whining! Fight for your*

parental rights, and never give up until you gain or restore
your responsibilities, your legacy!

For me, the legal challenge was a personal battle to
regain self-respect, as well.

I'm no slacker when I embark on a crusade of any
kind. I knew that whatever the courts decided would
change my life forever. I had a figurative bag of stones,
facing Goliath. But figurative or not, my crusade was
going to be a source of pride.

Gaining substantial visitation rights, however
logistically awkward or expensive, was my fiercest desire.
And I wanted to contribute my fair share of money to
support my son. The dispute rotated around first, finding
my son and then the money and time to share with my son.

We Latinos, after all, are known for our passion
focused on our blood kin, right?

Mama – my dear sweet Mother – had instilled in me
a desire for education and for a meaningful, better life. My
cliché faith in the American dream and fairness, justice and
the American way was still giving me hope.

But my quest would start out floundering in legal
quicksand, featuring short-sighted, often ignorant,
sometimes shady abogados/lawyers, including one former

district attorney and a woman-leaning legal system, grossly discriminatory to men.

I came to subscribe to Norman Mailer's cynical take on honor:

> *"Because there is very little honor left in American life, there is a certain built-in tendency to destroy masculinity in American men."* – Mailer, <u>Cannibals and Christians</u>, "Petty Notes on Some Sex in America," 1962-'63, 1966.

I fathered a child, out of wedlock. What a despicable crime! I was not proud of my achievement at first; it was very embarrassing. Another kind of "despicable me," and this was far from the animation of Hollywood.

In an almost knee-jerk reaction, I resolved to be the best father I could be, given the long distance gap and the mother's reaction to my efforts. The legal system, and the mother-to-be if she were truthful, seemed to think I was mounting a conspiracy of some kind. *My effort itself – to be a meaningful, engaged, effective part of my son's life – was, I felt, being cast as a despicable crime!*

The mere mention of doing battle in family court may lead some people to think that I am a deadbeat dad, trying to escape paying child-support and performing the other God-mandated duties of fatherhood. Yes, I believe that God, and one's own manhood, demand fathers to do their fair, just and loving duties.

If you read this book with the sole intention of finding a way out of supporting your children, then you have missed my heart. Pass the book on to someone else.

Children are so vulnerable and cannot provide for themselves! The _Bible_ teaches: "A man who does not provide for his family is worse than an infidel." I believe this wholeheartedly. But, religion aside, men are called by nature to care for their family.

Maybe I am naïve, but yes, I do believe that most men see **fatherhood** as an honor above and beyond and unlike any other. I cannot fathom how anyone can abandon a child or fail to provide – at the very least – life's necessities for a child. Apparently not a lot of dads agree with me. Dave Eberhart wrote for Newsmax about "Deadbeat Dads Enjoy Immunity from U.S. Laws", December 22, 2008, and cited the Federal Office of Child Support's last accounting of U.S. child-support payouts:

"$96 billion in unpaid support had accumulated and was due to U.S. children; 68 percent of U.S. child-support cases had payments in arrears; an overwhelming majority of U.S. children – particularly minorities – are living in poverty in single-parent homes where child-support checks or cash are not paid, not paid on time or not paid in full."

Some time ago, I heard the following song lyrics from the song titled "Because I Got High," as sung by Afroman:

I was going to go to court before I got high...they took my whole paycheck, and I know why, 'cause I got high. I was going to pay child-support, but then I got high."

I cannot conceive of having a more repulsive reaction to any song than I had toward those lines.

I grew up poor, in the "projects" in Puerto Rico, surrounded by criminals, drug addicts, fugitives of all kinds – yes, deadbeat dads, too.

I was the child of a chronic alcoholic dad.

I was the youngest of 17 siblings. At any given time of our lives, we had 10 of us together with our parents sharing a three-bedroom house with rotten wooden floors, holes in the roof, a typical place in the residential ghetto. Our part of Puerto Rico tended to be rainy often; so pots and pans commonly were strategically placed around the house to catch the leaks and prevent the wooden floor from further rotting. In our rather level neighborhood landscape, it was common for water to pool around and under our house, which was built on stilts to escape the slow-draining rainfall runoff. We just rolled up our pants and carried our shoes to wade through our yard and other yards and streets, heading to school. Sometimes we stepped on pieces of wood; we tried to make them steps as the water receded, but found ourselves often slipping, landing in the persistent mud! On days off from school, the flooded yard served as our *improv* swimming pool!

My father was middle-aged when I was conceived. I therefore came to know a retired old man as my father. Everyone thought he was my grandfather.

Dad was a brilliant man; he could navigate through several languages and even corrected my college algebra....all with a 5th grade education. He was under-employed throughout his life, working mostly selling bread and as a construction laborer – when he worked – but often not working due to the booze. After reaching the official qualifying age for Social Security, Dad received $89.00 per month. Yes, eighty-nine dollars, and that was in the 1980s! Fortunately for us, we also received public assistance in the form of food stamps.

As poor as we were, Mama somehow provided for our basic needs, and never once did we kids – the 10 of us at home – lack for sufficient food, shelter and clothing, plus access to an education. Our mother – Angela, and she was our ANGEL – spent long workdays performing all the house-cleaning tasks, washing clothes and doing other chores in other people's homes.

Those were the employable skills that our "country-girl" mother, Angela, had.

While Mama worked for us, our father spent all the money he could get, to buy booze. I guess you can say I have craved to be the father that my father was not.

Mama made it possible for us to attend school. Her efforts paid off with me, and I became *someone* in this earthly life – the professional in attitude at whatever I do, the entrepreneur and the dreamer that I am today. I've started an alternative high school for at-risk children who fail to do well in today's mainstream schools. I invented a physical fitness device called My Wearable Gym for which I hold a patent. I composed an award-winning song and produced a number of recordings of my solo singing performances, attended three American universities, have been awarded a Honoris Causa doctorate degree, was a child actor and wrote this award-winning book.

Proudly I state that there would be no need for prisons and police if every man had a mother like mine.

She awoke in me a fire that was once only flickering in the innermost parts of my soul.

In 2003, I met a woman from Eastern Europe; while she visited in the United States, we were introduced by her cousin living in Texas. We dated for a while and came to have an intimate relationship.

In late 2003, I was told that I was a father.

And just as proudly, I also state, I immediately initiated generous child-support payments, long before my paternity was confirmed. I supported her fully before the child was born.

She needed the money badly for a while because, just as she revealed her pregnancy, her boss unjustly and illegally terminated her employment. I sent her money for the child's and her needs over the ensuing two years. It wasn't enough for her. My court adventures came when the new mother decided I must pay more for the privilege of sharing regular time with the child she identified as my son.

She then vanished for years along with my son.

My efforts to locate my boy through international channels paid off as mother and child reappeared again. This time however, she sued me in an American court, meanwhile denying me the opportunity to hear from my child.

You can quote me: *When you punish a man by denying him access to his child, you cease to be a mother and a woman. This denial is as criminal as failure to pay child support.*

Sadly, the litigation was a waste of money and time and goodwill, and the woman learned to be a great mother and a woman as I learned, long distance, to be a father.

Yes, I started by serving as my own attorney, but that would change quickly. When a person is involved in an emotional battle, it is best to hire someone outside the conflict to assist in all the legalities, so that the trauma doesn't lead to legal mistakes, errors of judgment, injustice, more trauma, hatred. Even lawyers sometimes find another lawyer to represent them.

In 2009, more than five years after learning of the pregnancy, I succeeded in getting DNA proof that I was, indeed, the father of the European woman's child!

On April 26, 2009, my court battles appeared to end with a resolution. Or so I thought.

In the process, I became knowledgeable on family law applying to fatherhood, and learned how The Hague

International Criminal Court came to play a role in international fatherhood.

     In the end, I won a fair ruling from the court – or so I thought.

I wanted to support my child in all ways possible, but where was he?

Chapter 2 – *The word "fair" doesn't exist in our judicial system.*

My Judgment:

The word fair does not belong in a court of law, and judges have no obligation to be fair. They simply interpret and apply the law. The law itself may have been intended to deliver fairness in court, but there's never any guarantee.

*****

A bueno/good abogado/lawyer I met, one specializing in family law, a former district attorney, mentioned that I might be ordered to pay child-support without ever seeing my child and did advise that I get the word "fair" out of my head.

That prospect for me and my fathering responsibilities, of course, would not be fair!

If I expected visitation, the lawyer said, I would have to go to the international Hague tribunal.

In other words, in the United States, I might be ordered to pay child-support but might never see my child!

The U.S. court might turn me into a debit card for my one-time lover!

In the years that followed the conjugal results from our Latino-European affair, I became a pseudo-expert, or rather, an informed client, on family law as it applied to fatherhood. I learned how The Hague and a related international treaty came to play a role in international fatherhood. After all, I was counseled to channel my legal pursuit of visitation rights through the same court that prosecutes international criminals. *Wow, I thought, I'm just an everyday sort of guy, and I'm going to do battle at the International court, The Hague?*

My research, however, proved otherwise. Yes, this former DA-turned family law specialist was wrong. It was an example of legal malpractice with no money-back guarantee.

The Hague Court, I learned, is also the international court that provides a service to humanity by protecting children involved in international disputes. As such, it serves the nations that signed to be participants in the related treaty agreements. Cases of international abductions of children are one of The Hague's primary jurisdiction areas.

It appears, though, that The Hague does not interfere with local courts' jurisdictions over common family law disputes and cannot order visitation for parents in divorce, custody, child-support or most other parenting issues, including mine.

Of course, during the course of my jet-hopping romance with the European woman, as do many men, I never dreamed of complications. We had good times together, and then I thought it was over; I thought I had terminated our relationship.

NOT!

This one started with a kiss and ended with a lawsuit.

I thought the kiss would be forgotten and the love-making was over back in early 2003. Then suddenly, via that marvelous but now ancient "beeper" tech, I received a message – typed and channeled, the precursor of today's texting – bearing the news that my brief love affair had produced a pregnancy. She claimed. I was not sure though. We broke off our relationship and there was resentment.

As I read the message from the other side of the world, my hands seemed to melt as I was descending some concrete steps in Texas. I trembled and dropped my beeper. I kneeled to retrieve the plastic and metal pieces; maybe I should have prayed for divine guidance. I would soon plunge into my new world, a realm of emotions and legalese, frustrations and intense pride.

With all the steely-eyed passion of a banker demanding asset, collateral and planning documentation from a customer seeking a loan, I requested a pregnancy test, then paying for an ultrasound exam.

Soon I saw the electronic image that proved, she said, that she was pregnant. That I might be a father was both thrilling and chilling. I saw the first human pecan of a little boy forming in the womb! Still, I could not believe that I was extending my family's roots back to Europe, where my ancestors had come from.

Now, if she were truthful, there was the image of a *piece of heaven* incubating in the womb of a woman that I had loved physically – the consummation of an intimate relationship between a European female and a Puerto Rican male!

I still did not know if the child was really mine, but it didn't matter at that moment. I was happy just to know that I was probably no longer a solo player in this world. I would not be alone, I fervently hoped. Someone was here, now carrying my DNA.

I was ecstatic about the possibility of someone calling me "Daddy!" Maybe a live product of my own being, my blood and flesh, my DNA, was coming into this world.

Was this a dream!? I certainly felt that it was real. I was already fantasizing about what "Johnny" – I even had his name chosen, my namesake – would be, do, achieve, as he grew up. I had big plans for us spending a lot of time together. I aimed to introduce him to the father who loved him, though from a distant land.

You see, this new Johnny was born as I approached maturity, the new Johnny having been conceived in haste, by accident, sort of, without "a jimmy hat."

So, naturally, just in case I was approaching the last dim light of my existence, I sat down and wrote my Johnny a letter.

He was still an embryo at the time, but I wanted to write that letter so desperately, so passionately, so lovingly, intending that my son would know the basic truth about me and, I hoped, that I would pass along some wisdom that I had earned, learned, gleaned in my half a life on this earth.

I wrote to Johnny......

My letter:

"Dear Son,

"Johnny, when you grow up, you must learn about the young man I once was and the old man that I would become.

"I yearn to build a library for you, similar to the one we had when I was growing up, the shelving made of six boards, one for each side, top and bottom and two in the middle. It was a simple library from which I juiced the first glimpses of literature - poetry and prose.

"The youngest in a large family with 16 siblings, I benefitted from literary leftovers that my siblings discarded in the bookshelf once they finished a class. They were old, dilapidated books that awoke in me a fire that had been dormant in the innermost refuge of my young soul.

"I'd rather pass on to you knowledge, my dear Johnny, more than anything else in the world. After all, I brought you into a world filled with hurts and frustrations, suffering and disappointments, but also with joys and curiosities, love and art, learning and adventures. I know that you will also fall many times, hurt and be hurt. So I ask that you give me the chance to teach and recite with you the Lord's Prayer.... 'forgive us… as we forgive...'

"It is hard enough that you live in a distant land. Although modern advancements have made it possible to see each other and talk directly, live, often, it's very hard to be a good father as shimmering electrons on a screen.

"My duty as a father is to be here for you and to be present when you need me. I truly yearn to be with you forever, even knowing it cannot and will not happen. In place of this dream, however, I have developed the first-ever parental kit of crazy glue so I could get my lips stuck to your cheek for eternity. I have started to work out so, when you are old enough, we can do a one-on-one game of basketball… 'una cocinita,' as we used to call it; I am not going to let you whip me!

"I have written a few music notes and composed some songs so you know what I did on my spare time. I want you to know my world of notes, clefs, and how I mixed time and sound to produce music.

"Understand, you have gorgeous eyes and beautiful hair; I in turn am Latin with dark eyes and fading hair. So I want to include with this note a picture of what I looked like in my twenties as I am not going to allow you to steal the scene with your good looks; this is what you would look like in a few years.

"I do love you, Johnny, and wish you were here and also know that you will do great things as, Kids like you, go on to change the world!

"You are my life until the oceans run dry, until the stars in the sky fail to shine.

"As you grow older, don't forget that, every night you live with me in my dreams.

"Love,
"your Dad, Johnny Sr."

Now for posterity, long live the letter I wrote to my son!

*****

Do I sound like a father unwilling to support his child?

Before my quest to be a loving, hands-on father was to end, I would come to think that the laws of man had been contrived to ruin honorable men, to protect children.

I almost titled this book, "Ruin Honorable Men to Protect Children."

Chapter 3 – *How naïve could I be? Real life lawyers are not Matlock, The Hammer, Judith Sheindlin (Judge Judy) or José Baez (Casey Anthony Case)!*

As soon as I heard of the pregnancy, I began sending child-support money via Western Union. In most months, the sums exceeded $500.00. Additionally, I paid the pre- and post-natal expenses.

At times my contributions to the child's and his mom's well-being hit $1,800 a month. At first in this period of the saga, she needed the money and it was the right thing to do; it was the moral thing to do.

I was already trying to do the right thing before I encountered anyone in a judge's chair.

I continued my monthly support for two years and sent extra money for furniture, a more spacious apartment and all the necessities.

It was 2003 and after the birth, I visited Europe, and the new mother handed me the child. I held him in my arms for the first time.

Here was the Johnny I wanted, in my arms, warm and cuddly! Wow! The new Johnny and the old Johnny stared at each other for a time. Then I broke the news: "I am your father." We stared at each other... his eyes wide open, a gorgeous little boy. I think I made an impressively grand first impression on the infant, even if I did not sound like Darth Vader.

I had my fatherly joy of taking care of him . . . changing diapers, feeding him, reading to him, rocking him to sleep . . . being a new daddy. The mother made a video of me explaining to men how to change a diaper. She laughed and laughed until I realized I was trying to fit the baby with the diaper inside out...wonderful times. Indeed, it was my best of times. We had more grand conversations, though one-sided as they were or seemed. How can any father know for sure that he's not being understood, subconsciously or otherwise, by the infant?

I also produced a video of my infant son and almost daily added more to it before my joys of his babyhood were halted. More than 11 years later, when Johnny turned 12, we watched the video together....we laughed and we wept.

My boy has kept the video until this day. Soon he will be entering high school.

My vacation time was soon to end, and I had to leave Europe and my cherished offspring, my DNA in such a charming, cute, handsome son. But before my return to the States, I left an ATM card so the mother could withdraw funds as needed for the child's needs.

I trusted her judgment and must admit that she did not fail me or our son, not when it came to supplying his needs. And I also had done some fiduciary homework. At that time, monthly wages for a reputable attorney in Europe were around $1,000.00 a month. I also learned that the brother of a European acquaintance of mine was working as an apprentice lawyer for the government there. He was being paid $55.00 a month. Yes, I said, fifty-five dollars.

Much later, I would discover, Johnny's mother had become re-employed, without telling me, and was making *$300* a month – then a whopping sum for her cranny of the world -- working as a secretary/clerk for a law firm.

At that time, I was paying Johnny's mom $500.00 monthly, and I did not mind taking care of them both. I believed she needed the money. For my son's first birthday celebration, I sent the regular $500 for support plus $300 more for a birthday party. In essence, with what I contributed and what she earned, both mother and child were living very well.

There was no court order needed. No court order had been issued. I did it because I wanted to do it, and I could afford to do it…it was the right thing to do.

*****

My Judgment:

Regardless of any court order, favorable or not to you fathers out there, don't fail to provide for your child. *Tykes are so weak, trusting, impressionable, vulnerable!*

If you don't have money to give, try getting diapers, milk, clothes, baby formula, wipes… Get a job and pay for doctor visits— Do child care while the mother works. Visit a charitable organization or church that often hands out donated goods. Get something for the baby. Contribute something.

Sorry, but a "Go Fund Me" won't work here!

If the moral correctness doesn't lead you to do the right thing however, Judge Judy, that judge of the popular TV show, will remind you.

She's a family court/law judge. In a TV interview on family law, Judge Judy said:

> *"If you're going to try to make a fool of the justice system by not following the rules, by flaunting its orders, by not abiding by the laws of the place where you live, there is a consequence. I am your consequence."*

Judge Judy further declared that she had incarcerated many deadbeat parents after giving each of them opportunities to do the right thing.

And YES, a broke father who supports and spends time with his child carries more honor than a rich one that only sends checks.

It seemed so quick: As Johnny was aging toward toddlerhood, I found that I was unable to return to Europe. When my son was two years old, I asked his mother to come and bring him to the United States. I offered to pay all expenses, including at her request some additional money for a visa.

I sent all the money needed and requested – totaling some $1,200.

I awaited the visit, but the months rolled by, and she never brought the child and did not get a visa. The additional money was pocketed and spent in Europe. Some observers might call that action criminal. I thought like mom and child may have needed it, but I still felt cheated.

When I first learned that I was probably a father, I felt like a criminal.

Some of you readers may judge me as a "deadbeat dad" because I cut off my voluntary child-support payments after the mother decided she needed more money and denied me access to our child.

But I repeat to you, with all the sincerity and passion of a man determined to be a father that I agree with the Bible's teaching that a man who does not provide for the wellbeing of his family is "worse than an infidel." I never even flirted with a fleeting thought of leaving our child or his situation with his mother wanting for their needs and more!

Access to be my son's father was the core factor in my legal battle.

It's a long way from my home in Texas to him in Eastern Europe ... 5, 617 miles!

So, during the long legal process, yes, I was worried about that distance and the power of any court to enforce the Texas visitation/custody rulings on a European citizen/resident. What would happen should my son's mother decide never to bring the child to the United States for visitation, as was eventually ordered? According to two family lawyers that I consulted, nothing would happen to her. Texas and the United States have no "reciprocity" agreement with some Eastern European countries.

Therefore, the two lawyers said, the authorities – here and there – could not force her to adhere to a court order on visitation/custody.

On the other side of the parenting equation, however, the court here would likely take action on child-support issues stemming from the court orders. If I failed to make payments as ordered, and upon the mother's legal request, I face devastating consequences. The court, on the other hand and at best, could impose a fine on the mother– probably about a month's worth of child-support money. Maybe less.

Of course, the mother could always do it again a few months later, in the same court, or another court…and then again.

My worries proved to be partially justified although the realities could have been much worse.

On one occasion, after our case was decided, the mom arranged to bring my child for visitation but intentionally gave me the wrong date and time. She also violated the rules on location.

I wasted my time waiting at the airport.

I contacted her the following day, and she asked that I pick up the child. She would tell me where to pick him up.

She promised to send the details via text, which came about 10 p.m.

The details showed that she was staying at a hotel just a two-and-a-half-hour drive away; she further stated that she was leaving early the following morning on a trip and that I needed to pick up my son immediately.

I was frustrated, and of course, I was unable to do so in such short time.

I replied to her, advising that I would contact my lawyer in the morning because she violated the court order by taking my son out of state without my permission during my visitation time…. Yes, her playing around would cost me more money.

The following morning, she contacted my lawyer and delivered the child to my lawyer's office.

My consulting appellate attorney insisted that child-support and visitation rights be considered separate from each other. It meant that if I do not pay child-support, I still cannot be denied access and visitation.

Likewise, in turn, should the mother not allow me to see the child or if she denied me access and visitation as ordered, I'm still held responsible for paying child-support.

I mentioned to my appellate attorney that the court order in my case stated that the mother and the father, either or both, would suffer serious legal consequences for not obeying the orders. Maybe this was a departure from the normal practice, not sure?

The appellate attorney challenged me on this matter. He doubted that the court would try to reach out to the mother in Eastern Europe, to force her to adhere to the orders and/or to punish her.

I was surprised to find that an attorney with 20 years of family law practice would be unaware of the court's willingness to act, unless such moves are new in practice. I pulled out the court order and showed him. The pertinent order was in bold, capital letters on the last page of the legal document:

> *"WARNINGS TO PARTIES: FAILURE TO OBEY A COURT ORDER FOR CHILD SUPPORT OR FOR POSSESSION OF OR ACCESS TO A CHILD MAY RESULT IN FURTHER LITIGATION TO ENFORCE THE ORDER, INCLUDING CONTEMPT OF COURT. A FINDING OF*

CONTEMPT MAY BE PUNISHED BY CONFINEMENT IN JAIL FOR UP TO SIX MONTHS, A FINE OF UP TO $500 FOR EACH VIOLATION, AND A MONEY JUDGMENT FOR PAYMENT OF ATTORNEY'S FEES AND COURT COSTS."

One can assume by reading the court order that – should the woman not allow me to see the child and not bring him to the United States for visitation as ordered – the court, at my request, could suspend child-support. After all, what other recourse does the court have but withhold the check I write for her every month? The court sends those payments to her.

She was, for all practical purposes, in contempt of the court order on visitation. The court would have to make the decisions. But, as I learned, the worst that could happen to her could be getting fined by the court… So, she would be able to pay the court fine, with my money.

Should I decide to disobey the order, as well, I could face incarceration, regardless of the mother's actions.

If the order was not a two-way street, the court might not dispense justice.

There are many more potential nightmares for parents in parenting disputes.

Following the court's ruling in my case, my attorney shared that the state attorney general could re-visit my case and decide to increase the child-support amount and/or change other terms decided by the judge. Yes, the end is monetary – and it can make the court look tough.

I was told that numerous Texas cases are reviewed even when no late payments have ever occurred and even when no child-support recipient has requested a review.

I was truly disappointed by the prospects of no end to the court's involvement in our case and to the expenses required to defend myself.

I was instructed to account for every receipt for any money spent while exercising my visitation rights, in excess of my child-support outlay, just in case the attorney general decided to review our case.

REMEMBER: Once you decide to take your case to court, the court and the state take charge of the situation -- forever.

During my first visit with my child, in addition to child-support and the necessary travel expenses, I also incurred other related costs that exceeded $3,000. This expense is not calculated as support, and no credit was given to me. None will be given to you, either.

I was not much bothered by this situation, but similar practices can lead some people to go over the edge of reason, even insane.

In all, during the time span of three years prior to my legal adventure, I paid more than $20,000 in child-support and for pre-/post-natal care, and a planned trip – all without a court order.

My financial situation, income flow, meanwhile, changed for the worse. I suffered a back injury as the result of an accident and, with added medical bills and limited work, I had to reduce my monthly payment from $500 or more to $300; that was all I could afford and still pay my bills.

Regularly, I would call to talk to the baby as well as the mother.

Then, as the money amount changed, everything changed, almost overnight, it seemed. The mother's new responses became elusive and did not vary much: "I am not at home." "The child is asleep." Or simply, there was no answer… I often spoke to a dead phone. I was worried. Maybe something bad had happened to his mother, I wondered. If so, how would Johnny be cared for? Who would take custody?

I was finally able to reach her by phone, thank God.

I proceeded to request other contact information from her. I wanted phone numbers and/or names of individuals that I could contact about the child's health, care, wellbeing and whereabouts. I needed contacts in case something was to happen to her.

The woman who once wanted me to love her and marry her became a different person, I thought. She refused to provide the information.

I say this once again: When you punish a man by denying him access to his child, you cease to be a mother and a woman.

I concluded that she was hiding important and maybe even critical information related to our son. My worry escalated to the point where I was near panic, thinking that she might not even have possession of our child. A year later, I discontinued all financial support. I was emotionally destroyed—a part of me was gone.

With my legal efforts in Europe terminated and her demands for more money from me rising, the case would have to come to the United States. My early strategy, cutting off child-support, paid off; the woman from Europe would be forced to come to Texas, too. It was then that I started looking for a lawyer.

Listening to a friend's recommendation, as noted earlier, I contacted that Dallas-based lawyer licensed to practice law in the United States and in Europe. I provided the lawyer intimate details about my situation and personal information about the mother of my child. I assumed he was my attorney. Don't miss this tip: As soon as an attorney tells you that he is a lawyer and you confide intimacies of a case to him, he is bound by ethics to protect such information confidentially and cannot represent your adversary.

Also Eastern European by birth, the lawyer was surprised that he had never heard of this beautiful woman that I had found so alluring. He said he didn't know her.

The lawyer and I decided to get back in contact with each other soon, but then my employer sent me out of town. I was gone for a few weeks.

Upon returning, to my amazement, I was officially served with a child-support lawsuit on behalf of the woman who had once been my lover.

I was stunned to find that she was now represented by none other than the same attorney with whom I had consulted, and confided in, earlier! I was astounded to also learn – from the documentation presented to the court – that this same lawyer had listed his own mailing address as his client's, my ex-lover's, address.

Thus, if I paid more money to support my son, that money would first go to the lawyer who was first my attorney, then not my attorney. He did not inform the court that his new client did not reside in the United States. I figured that my child would never see one penny of my additional support if I sent it.

Unethical, I thought, an understatement, for sure. With his expertise, he could and probably would have destroyed the livelihood and ruined the life of the mother of my child if she challenged him over the money, if I had sent it.

I had become a victim of a shyster. At several Eastern European festivities that I attended locally in Texas, I learned that this villainous *abogado* had a reputation for questionable conduct with Europeans living in the United States and others living in Europe.

This shyster was not a family lawyer and did not correctly file court documents; those he presented did not meet the requirements of the State Family Code to establish paternity.

The judge, though, – here I found myself in a U.S. court – tried to apply the shyster's logic and tried to grant his request for the child-support and help him as much as possible. As said in other parts of this book, judges will try to fit you in. In a family court, you are guilty unless proven innocent. The judge flipped the papers multiple times as if trying to find a reason to oblige. But the errors in the submitted documents drew an easy verdict. My foe was not a family lawyer, and his documentation had errors.

Yet, the court is no law school and no place for teaching lawyers.

Here in the tale, you need some additional info from early in my adventure, when I had gone to Europe, just after my boy was born. I had then formally recognized my son. I did so by visiting the American embassy and filing the required paperwork; immediately, I received Johnny's passport and a birth certificate of an American born abroad. He became an immediate American citizen! The documents named me as his father. The shyster lawyer used that against me.

In the Texas hearing, this moronic lawyer presented those documents as proof of my paternity. But those documents, regardless of how valid they were in other venues, were and are not recognized by Texas as proof of paternity.

The shyster was not trained in family law…was unprepared. He faced a Mike Tyson and was out cold!

The case was dismissed, and I prevailed, in the first round of my legal fight. But this was no time to hang up the gloves. The fight wasn't over.

The first lawyer for the woman from Europe lost the first round! But I continued to be deprived of access to Johnny.

In this twisting tale, the woman judge noted that she "dismissed" only "until re-filing" occurred. The legal maneuvering would come back to haunt me once again, and then again.

I immediately reported the shady lawyer to the State Bar of Texas, seeking his disbarment.

I began to wonder how a woman who never contributed a single penny to my country suddenly had more rights in the very court that, as an American, my taxes helped to support.

Chapter 4 – A word about dealing with lawyers ...

I recently read an article published in March 2016 on the National Post's www.nationalpost.com titled, "Worst Kind of Custody Dispute Ends with $500,000 in Lawyer Fees, after a 36-day Trial!" *That's a hefty half a million dollars in revenue for the lawyers, in just 36 days!*

The father in the case earned $100,000 a year and the mother, $30,000. One can imagine the years it will take this couple to pay these legal fees. Worst of all, the money will not go to benefit the child. Stubbornness, bitterness, hatred, even fear and/or arrogance often overcome logic, common sense and the goodwill needed to compromise, and for their selfishness, vengeance and/or other irrational motivations, people will pay a hefty price.

Foolishness has ruined many a parent. In a battle where emotions run high, stupidity can set in, and a desperate moment may lead to financial disaster and mental anguish or, too often, violence against a loved one. Ruined marriages, estranged or plainly warring family camps, personal bankruptcies and even prisons have more than a fair share of otherwise good people who were blinded by evil in a flash.

One such case was featured on the TV show **_20/20_** a few years ago. It told of a man so fed up with a court's actions that he took his children and hid them.

Then he was jailed, and refused to reveal his children's whereabouts.

While incarcerated, he was visited by the children's mother, who tearfully pleaded with him to let her see the children or to tell her where the kids were located.

As if all hope were gone, the father replied:

"You did not care that I lost everything I had. Because of you, I lost my job, my career, my retirement savings, my home, my reputation, my freedom. You went after money and . . . did not care that I was your children's father. Why are you crying and pretending to be devastated? You got the money you wanted. You should be very happy. Go away and enjoy the money with your lover!"

Sure, it's contrary to any sensible judgment, but it does demonstrate how some people with hidden issues or plainly visible passions can be driven to extremes.

Rest easy. I am not advocating such extremes.

*****

My Judgment:

In a battle where emotions can easily rule, beware: *Don't bring your guns to town, son!* Don't tear you own spiritual house down. Those who hate you will never win, unless you hate them back. And if you do that, you will destroy yourself and probably others you loved or once loved. Often, the mind creates problems that do not exist. *Learn to master it!*

As I say often, a poor agreement/settlement is better than good litigation. Lawyers will tell you that they will try to avoid going to court at all cost and that they'd rather reach a reasonable agreement.

*****

I repeat: I consulted with nine different *abogados* who advertised themselves as family lawyers.

Lawyers have bills to pay just like the rest of us. Often, to attract sufficient clients to pay the bills and earn higher profits, a lawyer's advertising touts a variety of legal services and expertise, even in specialty areas of the law where they themselves may be deficient or potentially not

68

up to some clients' needs. So, after landing one of these high-maintenance clients, the lawyer will secure an attorney friend/associate who truly has the specialized expertise needed. That's no crime. But you might be paying two lawyers instead of one. Check your contract before signing: It could state, "for your case, I might require the assistance and services of another attorney . . . ." But of course, that would be a contract drafted by a lawyer to favor himself/herself. In fact, this arrangement might not be a bad deal if you trust your primary attorney; you could land a winning team. On the other hand, you may be able to cut your costs while hiring just the one lawyer with the skills/knowledge and expertise you need most.

None of the nine lawyers I consulted, however, had any experience in the law pertaining to international family law. Each simply followed the Texas Family Code guidelines of treating foreign countries as states. That's what I challenged.

I continued to read and research, aiming to choose my first attorney to actually represent me. I wanted a professional heavyweight, powerful and smart and specialized, and I wanted a female, to balance the gender issue in court action.

Five of these lawyers, including a former assistant district attorney (ADA), provided uninformed, poorly researched, unprofessional and/or inaccurate advice.

The former ADA advised that the court would order me to pay child-support but could not order the mother to allow me visitation with and/or access to my son. If I expected to obtain visitation rights and/or other contact with the child, the ADA warned, (as noted previously) I would have to channel my request through The Hague Court, yes, the same court that's designed/designated/authorized to conduct international criminal trials!

The Hague Court did not seem to be the right course for me; however, I did not give up. I continued my search and research.

Understand that lawyers, as do other professionals, make their money based on their time spent on the job. That's understandable. You've seen *The Good Wife* and *The Practice* or *Boston Legal,* and the commercials by the Texas Hammer, right?

What's not understandable or justifiable, however, are common misleading practices among some lawyers.

✶ ✶ ✶ ✶ ✶

Here are some too frequent examples of the realities:

1. **The rosy outlook** – You the plaintiff or defense
client are told by your prospective lawyer that you have a good case, that he/she can represent you successfully, that you will very likely win your case. You hire the lawyer as your attorney.

2. **The "retainer"** – He/she requires a "retainer," an up-front fee for services that likely will not be spelled out in detail or may be spelled out according to the lawyer's whims. This is not a contingency fee. A "retainer" is what it says, a fee fully retained even if you lose the case or even if your attorney delivers substandard, weak, poor or inadequate representation. Often, any foolish charge is added to make your retainer disappear: work by the receptionist, the stamps, copies, phone calls and other add-ons... *And shazam, retainer gone!*

I have never received money back on any retainer.

3. **The "tune" changes.** – At some point after handing over the retainer,

71

after the passing of some period of time supposedly spent by your attorney investigating your case, he/she may well break the sad news that your case is not as strong as previously thought, that little or nothing can be done to win it OR that you must fork over more "retainer" to do more of the work necessary for success. If you seek details and specifics, your attorney may talk in circles, giving you no straight answers. Your anticipated legal "knight in shining armor's" tune has changed.

4. **Your "knight" drops your case and you.** – You probably get no refund of any portion of the retainer. That becomes your cost for not having a winnable case. The rationale is strong: Do you want to spend more money on a losing cause? No, not a good idea, your soon-to-be former attorney advises with grim, resonating wisdom sliding off his/her tongue.

5. **The multiplying fees** – Some lawyers are less expensive per hour. However, they will bill for any and all phone calls to them, their office, their receptionist or their legal assistance. They will bill for emails and such. The "lower" fee disappears! Remember, competent is better than cheaper!

During my trial, the child's mother, under cross-examination, admitted to having hundreds of thousands of dollars in assets. After the trial, my lawyer made an interesting comment: "If her lawyer had known how much money she had, [the lawyer] would have had a feast!"

Yes, there are different fees for the not-so-poor as well. Unnecessary hearings, motions, petitions ... money getting drained. In my case, the mother's lawyer talked her into appealing the trial judge's decision even though she had zero chance of prevailing. In fact, her appellate lawyer did not even show up for the appeals trial.

If there is a way to juice your money, there are plenty of lawyers who will find it! They run a "for-profit" business.

*****

My Judgment:

When you meet with your lawyer, leave extravagance at home. Dress simply. Wear no jewelry. Do not drive to the office or court in an expensive new BMW. *The fees will go up if you do!*

I recommend you meet with the prospective lawyers and request/require a

detailed resume of credentials with specific cases handled in the pertinent area/areas of law for your case. Require pertinent references. Then get a list of expected and potential costs. And do all of this before hiring your chosen attorney.

Once you choose your legal counsel and work begins, submit your request in writing for all detailed costs being charged against your retainer. Get a detailed bill for every charge and feel free to disagree without becoming a pest. Above all, respect your professional lawyer. I am simply saying, "Trust, but verify."

You just might be facing a lawsuit years later for unpaid legal fees, and you will not recall the details of that distant legal business.

Here is a very good, detailed sample invoice I received from my appellate lawyer, late in my legal journey. Along with this invoice, and this is good lawyering, he also included a letter explaining all the charges:

■■

DATE	ITEM	HOURS	AMOUNT
12/8/2009	Telephone conference with client; prepare letter to client; review appellant's brief,	.80	220.00
12/9/2009	court letter and	2.00	550.00
	order	.50	50.00
	Prepare Notice of	2.00	550.00
	Appearance; prepare fax to attorney		
	Work on brief		
	Trip to Courthouse		
	Research	1.00	275.00

Prior to this invoice, I requested and received a nice discount. I guess he imagined himself in my shoes and sympathized.

My actual first round of legal action is a case in point. After I lost the shyster lawyer to my opponent, my first round of legal action really began.

Prior to my first appearance with my first loyal attorney before the Dallas judge, yep, in Texas, I had brought my case home – my first victory. I already suspected I was in for an expensive ride.

I chose my first U.S. attorney, the woman and I agreed on a $2,500 retainer as "THE TOTAL fee" – her words – and we went to a short, initial hearing in court.

The day before this Dallas County family court hearing, I called my attorney's office to confirm our hearing time for the following day. I spoke with the receptionist for 27 seconds.

Here's when I incurred the high cost of talking to my attorney's receptionist. Three days after the call, I got the $94 bill for that call! Do the simple math, and you will find that the call's cost translates to $3.48 per second, $208.00 per minute, $12,533 per hour, as mentioned earlier. The world's most expensive lawyer was getting ready to take me, even before things began.

Already, I was not feeling a lot of confidence, during my day in court, for sure.

In less than an hour, my hearing for paternity, visitation and reasonable child-support terms was dismissed. The results seemed to come down to my attorney saying to me: "You don't have to pay child-support now but will have to do so later; so let me have that money now."

My attorney soon phoned me.

She said I owed her lots of money to cover her work, performance. We discussed the issues, and I requested an invoice.

A few days later I received a bill for an additional $2,500, twice the agreed-upon amount. The total amount of time spent, I calculated, was close to 4 1/2 hours. Customarily, attorney fees run from $225.00 to $300.00 an hour.

Let's grant her top dollar, credit this lawyer with $300.00 an hour. Basic arithmetic on a simple calculator returns $300.00 times 4.5=$1,350.00. That's far from her demand of $5,000: $2,500 already pre-paid plus an additional $2,500!

*****

My Judgment:

What I did, and I also recommend, was to sit down and write a detailed letter to my

attorney, questioning the additional charges. In the letter, I demanded specific dates and times that we spoke or work performed other than what I already knew.

Yes, just as good lawyers do, I had also kept a log of phone calls, personal visits, length of times, etc.

I included this log with the letter. I wasn't a total fool!

*****

I was ready to challenge my attorney to a hearing before the State Bar of Texas, so that I could dispute some charges. And she would have to try to justify them. In such a hearing before the bar, contrary to civil cases, the attorney has the responsibility of disproving the client's accusations or claims—guilty until proven innocent. She knew that.

I never heard from that lawyer again.

She took my $2,500 retainer with no further billing or dispute. I was out more than she was worth, but at least I didn't fork over more. I learned a valuable, costly lesson.

*****

My Judgment:

Prior to and during your legal action, get involved in your case, but never pretend to be a lawyer. Let the lawyer be the lawyer. *Submit to the lawyer's guidance but hold his/her feet to the fire!* Above all, respect your lawyer. You need him/her.

Do as much reading and research as you can about your case, and present your findings to your chosen attorney; tell him/her that you are simply an informed client.

Remember, it is your case, and if you are not satisfied with your attorney's representation of your interests, your rights or your positions in the case, you can choose to dismiss your lawyer; she/he works for you!

You could do it by writing a note and saying something like this:

> *Please be advised that I am terminating our attorney-client relationship, effective immediately, and you are to cease working on any pending matters of or related to my case.*

As a courtesy, please instruct anyone to contact me directly if he/she wants to discuss my case or give information related to my case. I will contact you to discuss pending fees, if any.

When you dismiss your attorney, *please, please pay him/her what you justly owe!!*

On a final note, be kind to your lawyer; this professional will probably be the only person capable of defending you without believing you!

Chapter 5 – *I feared I was descending into the often murky, terribly uncertain, sometimes unjust realm of international child-support.*

The year was 2006, winter was approaching, and I needed to hurry. I had to reach Europe before the region's typically bitter winter. I found myself in Eastern Europe and preparing to go to court, aiming to locate the baby, the child allegedly my son. I wanted to believe he was real, to believe he was my son. I was ready, I believed, to be a father.

As I suspected and hoped, I came to discover that he wasn't actually missing, but was out of my reach. Between poor phone services and his mother it became impossible for me to use the phone to stay informed about the baby. I had previously enjoyed my one-sided talks with him via the phone.

She had never brought him to the States as she promised, as I had paid for her to do.

When I landed in Europe, to find out what was going on, I was the one who was lost, feeling lost.

When the legal process goes international, as was my anticipated challenge, a wannabe father can find himself staring into a strange and possibly untranslatable abyss.

Unable to speak the local language, I did something unusual. You see, I love salsa music and know that anyone else who loves salsa could be an instant friend. So, I located a spot called Salsa Dos, a club owned by a local celebrity, in my former lover's native land.

I stepped inside and uncovered a salsa class in progress. I immediately joined the class. They were thrilled to have a Puerto Rican salsero in the house; so I became an instant friend. In another turn of good luck, one of the dancers was a guy who spoke good English, and I immediately shared the reason for my visit; he agreed to be my translator.

I had a translator, and I already had located a local lawyer licensed to practice family law in that country. It didn't help that my European attorney wanted to charge his legal fees at American rates, and he didn't speak much English. I was soon representing myself in a European legal system that wasn't very helpful, either.

The European system had its own versions of time and justice; scheduling of hearings was sluggish. I feared the local judges would feel no obligation or responsibility to be fair, impartial, with an American being the plaintiff. Well, I was convinced, they didn't have to give any consideration or even lip service to adhering to the principles of the U.S. Constitution!

We know what's supposed to happen in the U.S. legal system.

As laws are implemented and legal action begins, the courts set and rely on precedents – earlier pertinent decisions by various judges in various courts. Judges are not supposed to make laws; the legislatures and the Congress are delegated that responsibility, authority. The jobs of a judge are to correctly interpret and apply the law in real life situations.

Thereby, we like to believe, our system is fair to all parties in litigation.

U.S. lawyers, however, as I have already shared with you, warned me about using the word "fair" when dealing with our family courts. "Fair" should never be voiced or written or emailed or texted, they said. The concept is not part of the court's vocabulary, I was told.

I could not, would not, bring myself to give up my hope for justice. I, therefore, substituted "justice" wherever and whenever I would have otherwise have used "fairness"

– most of the time. But as the late comedian Richard Prior would often joke: *"If you step into the world looking for justice, you'll find "just us"…yes, you and me!*

As many people tend to believe, being male and hoping to get justice in a family court may be a losing cause, and the male will most likely be at a serious disadvantage when going before the judge. Or, so I thought! The cards are stacked in favor of the mother of the children. Everyone knows that, don't they? So I thought.

Not surprisingly, my experience in the courts and my research showed that – in the best interest of a child – judges *WILL FIND* a reason to order child-support money be paid. *It will happen* even if the judge has to cite a statute that does not directly apply to the circumstances or realities of the case. Child-support, superseding any other debt, is as close to a 100-percent certainty as anything in the legal system.

*****

My Judgment:
Now keep reading and see that, while embroiled in a paternity or child-support lawsuit, a man can be judged guilty until he proves his innocence. And proving that

innocence can become an unrealistic burden. Justice may elude the papa and the process.

*****

I had the rather naïve thought that perhaps the European and U.S. embassies could bring justice to my case. But embassies, I learned, are not equipped to handle civil parental disputes. A look at the U.S. consular Website on the U.S. Department of State home pages will open a window of information about embassies. A simple search on "child support and American embassies" will bring up the following statement:

> **"The U.S. Embassy is sometimes contacted by the (foreign) mother or father of an American child . . . requesting assistance in collecting financial support from the other parent in the United States. The Embassy is also sometimes asked to locate the absent parent for the purpose of collecting financial support. The Embassy regrets that it is unable to directly assist in these matters. In the United States, each individual state or territory maintains its own agency that is responsible for the administration of child-support. These agencies are not a part of the U.S. federal government, and for that reason**

85

they do not have representatives at the U.S. Embassy."

In short, embassies are not family courts or family law enforcement entities.

As the quote from the State Department Website indicates, each separate state or territory in our country is responsible for administering the laws and legal system related to child-support. And if you want to win custody of an American child or visitation rights or seek child-support or contest legal issues or court decisions involving a child, you go to the family court with jurisdiction, authority, over the issues and the involved U.S. resident parent. If you want to seek child-support for a foreign resident child sired by or given birth to by an American, you do the same. The U.S. case is filed in the local family court with jurisdiction over the U.S. resident parent involved in the case.

As the realities of the justice system show, I also was to learn that any woman from another country may fly to any U.S. city and file a paternity or child-support suit on behalf of her child. She may hire an American attorney without setting foot in the United States and file suit against you.

It is that easy! *And I would come to be very grateful for that reality!*

86

The reverse scenario, though, is not so easy. If an American woman should find herself pregnant by a foreigner who then returns to his country, that American has little or no recourse to secure child-support from the foreign-born father – regardless of the court's orders.

A woman friend of mine from Mexico, and this is a good example, ironically and unfortunately, was educated in the rude realities of such a case: She moved to the United States with her husband and their newborn child; she and the child became legal U.S. residents. After a few years, the marriage broke apart. Her husband returned to Mexico, where he became employed by a good company and also opened his own business. My legal U.S. resident friend filed for child-support, and the U.S. state-level family court with jurisdiction rightfully granted her custody and the child-support she sought. The court sent a petition to Mexico to have the husband's wages/income garnished for the child-support granted, and the money was to be forwarded to the mother.

The issue is that Mexico at the time was not signatory (It is today but good luck getting anything) to international agreements that, on paper, would have made it a country with a reciprocating relationship with the United States on matters of child-support. Therefore, this mom –

after 20 years of effort – has never received a penny of child-support from her Mexican husband!

No way, Jose!

In a similar case involving child-support and Mexico, and this one seems inconceivable. An American man was ordered to pay child-support for his two U.S.-resident children. Instead of paying, he moved to Mexico. According to this story published on Newsmax on Monday, December 22, 2008, the man's income was $975,000 a year, and he was ordered to pay $11,000 a month for his two special-needs kids. But rather than supporting his kids, he fled to Mexico.

From there, the story goes, he has his well-paid lawyer repeatedly file absentee nuisance complaints against his American former spouse, and she must respond or face contempt charges.

As of this writing, she's on the brink of bankruptcy while having to work minimum-wage jobs. It was also noted that she is close to having her house foreclosed upon.

(http://www.newsmax.com/US/deadbeatdads/2008/12/22/id/327264/#ixzz41VIyNDvS)

Yes, money can control the legal system, in some situations.

That's a sorry story of bitterness and rancor that, perhaps, could have been avoided. But the legal stage with lawyers fighting "for you" and for your spouse often creates this kind of hatred with that old "us vs. them" attitude. Parties to a family lawsuit can sometimes agree, but often here comes the "wise" or "wise-ass" or "super star" lawyer who blocks any reasonable agreement in pursuit of a lopsided settlement, more and more of whatever for his/her client. And both parties, who originally desired to work out their differences in the best interests of the children, end up as adversaries, forever. The children, though, tend to suffer most.

Again, money can beat or whipsaw the system.

I ran into a story published on July 2, 2017 in MSN Entertainment about singer and composer Paul Anka. The article titled "Paul Anka Wins Custody of His 11-Year-Old Son" tells of Anka winning the case against his ex-wife and gaining custody of his son Ethan. His ex-wife, former Miss Sweden Anna Aberg, was barred from having any contact with the boy.

Ethan had not seen his mother in more than two years, according to the article, and purportedly dislikes her.

Anna's attorney didn't mince words and said the "Lonely Boy" singer only won because of his wealth and prominence.

"His reported income is about $300,000 a month," the lawyer was quoted as saying. "He's been able to out-lawyer a woman who doesn't have the finances or the celebrity to combat him." Money did it!

*****

My Judgment:

Our laws are like no other in the world, but here in our own backyard, so to speak, we Americans have often received unfavorable judgments when sued by foreign citizens. In many cases, Americans have lost their homes, their livelihoods and their life-savings.

But just try suing in another country!

Should you prevail, you will receive two goats, four chickens and a horse with tuberculosis . . . at a phenomenal legal cost! I exaggerate, perhaps, but not much and it may take years to settle the case.

*****

But don't feel too bad.

The oil spill that ruined the Gulf of Mexico in 2010 and caused billions of dollars in losses to the local economies and environmental degradation is still being litigated, after 16 years. *Hang in there!*

And the poisoning of hundreds of thousands of residents by the Union Carbide plant in Bhopal, India – considered the world's worst industrial disaster – took 30 years to resolve. At worst, the parties at fault received two-year prison sentences and paid $2,000.00 fines.

On the other hand, an honorable American parent of a child may have to pay 100, 200, whatever times that for child-support and lawyers. And if that parent doesn't pay up, and on time, he or she can be incarcerated. Well, in the world we've known, that nearly always means the father.

In my case, I discovered there was no applicable international law or treaty or agreements or legal precedents – or any guidelines of any kind – that would pertain to a family law/child-support dispute between a citizen of Eastern Europe and me, a U.S. citizen and Texan.

The State of Texas has its own reciprocal family-law agreements with at least 11 foreign nations, but also did not and does not have such an agreement with some European countries, including the Eastern European nation where my alleged son was born and lived.

If an agreement had been in place, I believe there would have been a serious credibility gap concerning that country's legal system and its approach to family law and parental rights. I believe the U.S. government would find it impossible to recognize family law practices in most of Eastern Europe. The chances for U.S. relations there, I thought, were slim to none for reciprocity on parenting responsibilities.

Reciprocity for the United States, I learned, works if the other country establishes a reliable, trustworthy system for collection of child-support. That means that a reciprocal country establishes an effective system to collect child-support from the non-custodial parent. For the benefit of an American, the United States would do the same. That's reciprocity.

*****

My Judgment:

Few countries have entered reciprocal family-law agreements with the United States, but often when that does happen, the agreements have come to be worth little more than the paper that they're written on. Reciprocity must be equally respected, honored, in the nations that are parties to the agreement – in order for the process to work for the child and for the parents.

If a man from the United States or from a properly reciprocating country were to sire a child with an American woman and then try to escape his responsibilities by running to that reciprocating country, that nation's government – by treaty – could and should garnish his wages and even apply incarceration should he fail to support his child living in the United States. That outcome is a real possibility for an American man trying to escape his U.S. parental responsibilities by fleeing to such a foreign land.

Some European countries have no such reliable or equitable system. At best, it's one of the world's weakest tools for protecting children.

You can readily see why I had many reasons for nightmares, fears, over my expected international case. Was I the father? I was already acting like a father. If I was, how could I maximize my fathering efforts?

A few months into my litigation fight, as it evolved in Texas, I located a Fox News/Associated Press article published on March 23, 2009, of a news account of some European nations allowing consensual incest. Decriminalizing incest among consenting adults is allowed in parts of Europe as part of a range of changes, so-called "reforms" were installed in some criminal codes. Portugal,

France and Spain do not prosecute consenting adults for incest! The conclusion, apparently, held that not everything that is immoral has to be illegal. Or, possibly, a father who had been raping his little girl could be allowed to marry her once she grows up. I could just imagine such barbarism.

Seeking justice in a system like that might be considered pointless or naïve. We know how the deplorable act of incest can yield tragic genetic, medical, social and emotional/psychological effects/impacts. After all, how can it be explained to a child that his/her father is also his/her grandfather? *How could a rational national government be considering the legalization of consensual incest in any situation?*

A reciprocal agreement on child support or any family law matter might be impossible under such circumstances, I theorized.

On the other hand, because my former lover never raised any morality issues and never invoked her country's law in her family law case, I was sometimes optimistic about winning my side of our dispute – that I would be allowed to be a father to my supposed child and that I would pay a fair and reasonable level of child-support money.

Being an international dispute, I expected, my case offered scary prospects. I was tempted to seek custody, but I soon decided against that path. Just winning the right to be a father, albeit long-distance father, looked rather uncertain.

Another story on the international level sealed my decision against seeking custody.

In 2009, ABC News reported on Michael McCarty's struggle to convince the Italian government to return his son. Mr. McCarty had been in a custody battle with his son's mother, an Italian citizen living in the United States, and an American court had declared the boy's mother unfit. Mr. McCarty was granted full custody of his son.

That's when Mr. McCarty's nightmare began. He learned that his boy had been removed from kindergarten and taken out of the country to Italy. Apparently the mother petitioned the court in Italy to grant her custody. The Italian court also declared the mother mentally unfit.

Then adding irony on irony, without contacting any living relatives, the Italian authorities placed the child in an orphanage in Italy.

Mr. McCarty went to Italy and presented the court a warrant from the FBI for the mother's arrest on abduction charges. Mr. McCarty also presented the certified U.S. court order granting him custody and the court decision declaring her unfit. Most importantly of all, and surely expected, Mr. McCarty also had the backing of The International Hague Convention and treaties. And, yes, Italy was a signatory to the Hague Treaty on child abduction!

Almost incredulously, the Italian court – as reported in the media – refused to honor the American court's decision and did not allow the documents from the FBI and The Hague Convention to be considered in the case.

As of this writing, and after years of exhausting all recourse, Mr. McCarty appeared to decide that he needed some government official of high, impeccable, influential authority to bring about a just resolution.

*****

My Judgment:

International treaties cannot be entirely depended upon by anyone to render justice in custodial cases.

Mr. McCarty's son was in Italy as the result of a crime being committed, a child abduction. It was an international crime; thus, the international criminal authorities

and the FBI or U.S. Marshalls ought to be able to handle the case and bring the guilty to justice and the child back to his father.

NOT SO! The individual has to fight for himself.

Perhaps the unfathomable Italian judge in the case turned the whole episode into an opportunity to carry out a vendetta against the United States of America. Regardless, the Italian rulings seemed rooted in just one principle – stubbornness. Maybe it was a case of territorial pride, or a judge on a power trip.

Mr. McCarty will have to spend more enormous amounts of time and money to have justice served. He could be ruined financially and emotionally.

I wonder about The Hague Court, its effectiveness. Where is The Hague in all of this?

Where are the international treaties, those supposedly to be respected and followed by member countries? Are individuals expected to take matters of justice into their own hands? It seems easier to locate and repossess an automobile than to return an abducted child to his parents! For Mr. McCarty, however, that reciprocity did not seem to matter.

*****

The idea of channeling my request for visitation rights to The Hague Court did not fit me and seemed absurd. Italy had and has a reciprocating agreement with the United States; my "other country" did not and does not.

In my case, I found myself before a Texas associate judge who failed to deliver fairness, justice, desired practical results. So, I would come to appeal to the senior judge.

Yes, what I was reading in the press about international family lawsuits was giving me pause, cause to worry, more distress, the jitters, anxiety.

I read a report on a wholly domestic case focused on child-support, a case rampant with irony: Another article in 2009, released by the Associated Press, ran under this headline: "Man Jailed for Not Supporting Someone Else's Child."

This litigation targeted Frank Hatley, a Georgia man.

Mr. Hatley spent more than a year behind bars for failing to pay child-support – restitution to the state, that is, for past unpaid support – for a child who was NOT his, biologically speaking. The court, according to news reports, had known for more than eight years that Mr.

Hatley had no biological chance of being the father of the child.

Mr. Hatley, at age 50, was released from jail. Ultimately, basically though not wholly, he won his battle. But it was a long one even after two DNA tests confirmed that he was not the father. And the state itself has become the deadbeat.

Mr. Hatley's tale dates to 1986, when he was in a relationship. The woman became pregnant and gave birth; she told Mr. Hatley that the newborn was his son. Mr. Hatley believed her for many years. The two adults were never married to each other and did not live together, according to court documents, CNN and other venues reported.

The woman applied to the state for public support of her child after he turned two years of age, and that same law gave state authorities the right to pursue repayment of that assistance.

Mr. Hatley was the target, allegedly being the non-custodial parent and a deadbeat dad.

He responded by making reimbursement, support, payments – as possible – to the state for 13 years. He even forked over money from some unemployment checks.

Then, with the DNA results and the boy in his teens at the time, the court relieved Mr. Hatley from ongoing obligations to continue making child-support payments – **BUT NOT** from obligations to make past overdue payments.

He was assessed more than $16,000, money that he was previously ordered to pay prior to the state ruling and failed to pay. It was to be a reimbursement, at $200 per month, to the state for public money paid to the mother for the support of Mr. Hatley's previously alleged son.

The court was aware that the boy was not Mr. Hatley's son, according to news reports and court records.

But Mr. Hatley had earlier signed an official state document that would cost him a lot of money.

An attorney for Mr. Hatley told CNN much later that the court ruled Mr. Hatley liable for the past-due reimbursement because he had signed that agreement with the state's child-support services office. That document, Mr. Hatley's alleged consent, meant he had to make full reimbursement *for the years in which he believed that the boy was actually his son.*

Really? Ruin Honorable Men to Protect Children? In this case, one that's not his!

Mr. Hatley tried to comply, as much as possible, according to reports.

Still, in 2006, he spent six months in jail for falling behind on state-reimbursement payments of the money that went to the mother of the son that was not his. The man was described as hard-working and diligent; he stopped making the payments after losing his job.

Once again employed, Mr. Hatley restarted making payments and continued to do so until he was laid off from another job.

News reports later cited state records showing Mr. Hatley becoming homeless, living in his car while unable to make full payments. He went to jail in June 2008, despite his good intentions at trying to pay the money. He reportedly had paid $6,000 or more of the $16,000-plus.

Overall, Mr. Hatley made payments for about 20 years, until the non-son had become 20 years old.

Mr. Hatley's legal responsibilities did not end in 2008 – despite the paternity findings, despite his poor financial condition. Georgia Superior Court Judge Dan Perkins ordered Mr. Hatley to make the back payments!

In addition to CNN and AP and other reports, Mr. Hatley's story as cited herein includes information from the Southern Center for Human Rights' Website, https://www.schr.org/action/resources/falsepaternity, and from the paternityfrauddna organization's website, http://www.paternityfrauddna.com/tag/frank-hatley/.

It was reported on CNN that attorney Sarah Geraghty, a Southern Center for Human Rights lawyer, won Hatley's release.

A court order also finally relieved him of his ongoing financial obligations – past and present and future – to the Georgia Department of Human Resources.

"State child-support officials have shown extraordinarily poor judgment in Mr. Hatley's case," Geraghty was quoted as saying in one news report.

"We're satisfied with the result for Mr. Hatley, but still troubled by the state's monumental lapse of judgment in this case," the attorney was quoted telling CNN.

*****

My Judgment:

Sometimes, states in trying to impress, go overboard and ruin lives.

I was not surprised by Mr. Hatley's experience. Above all, the state's interest is served by making a definitive public impression on how much child-support is awarded/collected and by making a dramatic

public statement about fathers who do not pay child-support. Again, the system's focus is strictly monetary, as if it solves everything for every child.

With the government pursuing this passion above all other interests, however, honorable men can be ruined in their efforts to protect children!

In my view, the state still owes Mr. Hatley thousands of dollars and with interest.

*****

Although he was released and finally relieved of restitution, Mr. Hatley's paternity case is still not fully resolved, media reports indicate.

To my knowledge and according to reports, he has not been reimbursed for all that money he paid to the State of Georgia.

I also read about the millions of dollars that States brag about collecting in child-support, mostly from real deadbeat dads, thankfully. I have yet to read a report, though, on the number of children being reunited with both of their parents, the parenting triumphs, numbers of families uniting or reuniting, or the numbers of parents who have gained the right to visit, to be active/nurturing parents.

The Fort Worth Star-Telegram, in a Sunday article, "Inside Public Safety," page 5B (Nov. 2, 2008), reported then Texas Attorney General Greg Abbot, now the governor, boasting about "raking in the cash" from parents who were delinquent on child-support.

Abbot apparently directed the OAG Child Support Division to more aggressively pursue child-support "evaders" while publishing their names, addresses and places of employment.

According to the story, the child-support division was ranked first in the nation for the amount of money collected from deadbeat parents.

But based on my experience with the system and research findings, some of that collected money probably comes from "evaders" who did not owe it or who had their monthly payment rates raised, quite possibly without justification or fairness!

Regardless, there are other potential nightmares for parents in the child-support system.

Following the court's ruling in my case, my attorney shared that the state attorney general could re-visit my case and could decide to increase the child-support amount and/or change other terms already decided by the judge.

I was told that numerous Texas cases are reviewed even when no late payments have ever occurred and even when no child-support recipient has requested a review. And when support-paying parents ask for a review of their payment rates, the state can be slow or even refuse to grant the reviews.

Some of the money raised by Abbot's crew might have come as the result of reviews of cases where parents had faithfully and promptly paid child-support for years, those cases being ones in which the attorney general's office had decided to increase the payment obligations. After all, sadly too often, the best interests of the child and cultivating a healthy relationship between parents are superseded by the pursuit of a tough court image. The process has often come to being about the amount collected, not about the needs and wellbeing of the children and parents!

*****

My Judgment:

The more money raised, the better the court image. It's too often politics, not justice or wellbeing. Are the authorities not considering the possibility that divorced or separated mothers and fathers may have

moved on from the court experience and are satisfied with their child's financial wellbeing and are happy?

If we're hoping for a wise and fair process to make needed changes, the authorities would meet with father and mother and mediate or order a reasonable agreement. Check out the possible new circumstances.

If the agreement remains fair and effective, then why direct changes? *In other words, if it ain't broke, leave it alone!*

*****

"Out of it all, I just feel like justice should be served for me in this case," Mr. Hatley told *The Atlanta Journal-Constitution* shortly after his release in 2009. "I shouldn't have to keep being punished for a child that is not mine."

Sadly, in most states, I learned, a lawsuit cannot be brought against the woman or the state to recoup money wrongfully awarded to a plaintiff.

Now, we do take note that the State of Georgia is headed toward serving justice in the case of Mr. Hatley and wrongful outcomes in cases of other men.

"New Georgia Law Requires Genetic Testing in All Title IV-D Cases," according to an *Our Blog* installment, June 19, 2015, by Robert Franklin, a member of the National Board of Directors for National Parents Organization. It's a nonprofit aiming to educate the public, educators and legislators on the importance of shared parenting and advocating fair child-support and alimony legislation.

"Finally!" Mr. Franklin wrote, "The State of Georgia has taken a simple and obvious step toward sanity in its system of child-support enforcement." The step became law July 1, 2015, requiring "the state's child-support enforcement authority to genetically test any man named as the father in a Title IV-D case." Such cases involve mothers who have received Temporary Assistance to Needy Families benefits; when applying for said benefits, each mother is required to name a man as father. The man named is required to reimburse the state for what sums the mother received from the state.

Mr. Hatley almost certainly would have not suffered the injustice he did if the law had been in place ahead of his legal problems.

*****

My Judgment:

Remember, the word "fair" does not exist in the legal system. "Justice," sometimes, is also not found!

And so it goes that courts sometimes do err in the cause of justice, and it is up to you the defendant or plaintiff to show the evidence, challenge the injustices or errors and go after the facts. The case of Frank Hatley demonstrates a legal system, though passionate in its intent, flawed in some ways to its core.

If you don't have the finances to fight the legal battles, you could indeed be doomed!

On our part, we possible and wanna-be fathers need to corroborate and verify. Regardless, caution is the rule for any man who suspects that he is an absentee father.

*****

In another case – one reported by WFAA-Channel 8 News on Aug. 27, 2009 – there came a disturbing story of an 18-year-old man who received a letter from the State of Illinois Justice Department's child-support division demanding a retroactive payment of $16,000.

According to the detailed letter, Chad Covington had a 12-year-old child whom he had failed to support. The child's age, however, should have told the court that Mr. Covington was only 6 years old at the time the baby was born and, therefore, could not have been the child's father. For the previous six months, Mr. Covington had half his paycheck garnished to pay on the child-support debt. Court officials assured Mr. Covington that they did not send the letter and could not stop the garnishment!

They passed the buck, "not our problem." "Try the attorney general", that was the message. Or was it pure fraud from some prankster?

Government entities can try to pass on taking action even when it is "their problem." A few months ago I reported a theft at our office in Fort Worth, Texas, and a police department representative called me and took the information. "A detective will be contacting you soon," she stated. As months went by without a word from anyone, I went on the department Website and located the final word on the report. Surprisingly, the clerk noted on the report "not in Fort Worth." The "buck" doesn't always stop where it's supposed to.

Well, I guess some cities report low crime in their neighborhoods by that simple notation, "not here."

My Judgment:

Were they kidding in Illinois? *They were the justice enforcers! NOT!* **At a minimum, this court should have assisted Mr. Covington and forward this case to the fraud department.**

Unfortunately, in this age of fraud and identity theft, mistakes such as the one hitting Mr. Covington will be made for as long as there are human beings.

Now we have a new tool for truth, and hopefully the American way.

We are relying on DNA testing to resolve paternity.

In this sperm-and-egg-banking world of parenthood, DNA tests have revealed some amazing, even incredible genetic links. Yahoo News reported, in October 2015, that one man's own unborn twin brother was the genetic father of the man's son.

"Dad Learns That Unborn Twin 'Fathered' His Son," read the headline on reporter Neal Colgrass's story. Other stories about the strange case appeared in *The Independent*, *The Daily Beast* and *BuzzFeed*. A fertility clinic had aided the conception of a son for a U.S. couple.

110

The son had a different blood type from his purported parents. The son and the intended father had DNA that did not match despite the sperm coming from the wannabe father. Ancestry tests revealed that the bloodline father was the unborn uncle, Colgrass reported.

The dad/uncle proved to be a "human chimera," meaning the wannabe father had acquired genes of a twin brother who had died in the womb. The dad/uncle had passed those genes to the offspring via his twin's sperm.

Human chimerism, turns out, is not a new phenomenon and may even be common. Discovering this "trick" of nature, though, is rare because DNA testing is called upon only when there's cause for doubt, suspicion, of paternity or during a legal battle over custody or child-support. And such test results also leave a small chance that the intended father is the real father. And it can be argued that the real father is the man who impregnated the mother or provided the semen for the fertilization, regardless of the genetic provenance.

Naturally, we should not be surprised when accurate DNA testing may not be the decisive paternity factor.

In another strange case, this one out of the State of Michigan, a man was ordered to pay support for a child despite DNA testing that proved the child was not his, biologically.

Frank Hatley's case does not stand alone in this category, but there are additional wrinkles in Carnell Alexander's case, as reported in several Website stories, including one in *The Week Magazine*, online at http://theweek.com, and another on the National Parents Organization Website.

The news reports agree on details:

- Mr. Alexander's ex-girlfriend gave an incorrect name when she tried to name Mr. Alexander as the father of her child in the early 1990s, but she, nonetheless, received Temporary Assistance to Needy Families. A social worker had told her that she had to provide a name to receive income assistance.

- Another wrinkle, this is a case of goofs. The State of Michigan aimed to sue Mr. Alexander for child-support, but it failed to notify him of the lawsuit against him; the state's notice of suit was mistakenly given to a relative of Mr. Alexander. Because Mr. Alexander was in jail at that time, he can prove he never received the notice of the lawsuit filed.

- Just one more problem: Mr. Alexander was not the father, as DNA testing has subsequently proved, according to "Man Ordered to Pay Child Support for a Child That's Not His," an article in *The Week Magazine*, "Speed Reads," October 28, 2014.

Unfortunately, the State of Michigan did not seem to care about that detail or the other miscues. It has embroiled Alexander in a paternity case going on for years, probably driving him to financial and emotional ruin.

The DNA evidence and ensuing testimony of Mr. Alexander's ex-girlfriend both agree that he should not have had to pay a dime to support a child that wasn't his, but Michigan insists that he still owes about $30,000.

Mr. Alexander has refused to pay and has been threatened with jail time as a result. With certainty, it is my opinion, he will spend time in jail.

The child in question, meanwhile, is now in his late 20s, *The Week* reported.

To further complicate matters, the court handling the battle for several years has not had jurisdiction over Mr. Alexander, according to the Website story in **Our Blog**, headlined "Carnell Alexander Update: As Predicted, an Attorney Appears," Nov. 10, 2014, by Robert Franklin, a

113

member of the National Board of Directors of the National Parents Organization. The story can be read at https://nationalparentsorganization.org/blog/22037-carnell-alexander-update-as-predicted-an-attorney-appears.

The explanation provides good material for law classes, as well: Courts are subject to two legal definitions of "jurisdiction." A court has jurisdiction of case, Mr. Franklin says, if the court is given jurisdiction over the subject matter of a case and jurisdiction over the person who is the defendant in a case – read that again, you might have missed it.

"The court that's ruled in Alexander's case had jurisdiction of the subject matter, i.e. child-support, but none over Alexander since he was never properly informed about the case against him," Mr. Franklin states. "The original child-support order is therefore null and void because a court without jurisdiction is a court whose orders are without effect."

Mr. Franklin's comments continue: Mr. Alexander apparently was unaware of the legalities, and his "efforts to right the wrong done him have been in vain." Since this story started airing in public, however, Mr. Alexander has found another, apparently more astute lawyer to "fix" his legal mess. It is something he couldn't afford before. The new attorney, Cherika Harris, has been working to get justice for Mr. Alexander.

Nonetheless, Mr. Franklin thinks it is possible that the state will not go after the real father, a man already known and already having a long relationship with the child. Still to be determined, will the state continue to seek $30,000 in payments from Mr. Alexander? One claim by the state holds that "Alexander voluntarily subjected himself to the court's jurisdiction by failing to challenge the original order on that basis. In essence, the state may say he agreed to the court's jurisdiction."

*****

My Judgment:

Mr. Alexander could and, I believe, should win the case.

In this case, the state has relied on a child-centric approach. The needs of the "child" outweigh fairness when the real father cannot be found. Again, "fair" does not exist!

This story reminds me of a time when I worked at a supermarket as a bag boy during my high school days. A few customers complained of being shorted on merchandise whenever the bag boy assisted in carrying the groceries to their car. Accordingly, a few co-workers were fired even though they were absolutely not at fault! As in Michigan, my former boss used the "we-need-to-blame-someone" approach and fired the workers who at that moment happened to be standing in front of him.

Thus, extrapolating, if the needs of the child outweigh fairness, someone will be tagged as the father!

The unlucky man so labeled then must show that he's not the father and spend himself flat, depleted, broke – both emotionally and financially.

The State of Michigan adhered to a classic legal position, a "loose family law" doctrine.

I'm convinced the woman should be ordered to reimburse the state and/or Mr. Alexander. She was lying, initially. Mr. Alexander probably lost his job, the means to earn his livelihood, his reputation. He would likely have been unemployable as a former convict. His credit-worthiness rating probably sank as his delinquencies on paying child-support, as ordered, were reported to credit bureaus.

A man was ruined!

Would be wise for the State of Michigan to follow the State of Georgia's lead and make DNA testing a requisite when a father is identified by a mother seeking state aid for child-support.

****

"The new Georgia law means that there will be no Carnell Alexanders in that state," Mr. Franklin said in his June 2015 *Our Blog* online via the National Parents Organization Website. "In short, the State of Georgia has done what every state should do – take steps to ensure that men named as fathers actually are fathers and those who aren't fathers aren't burdened with supporting a child who's not theirs."

Failures to pay child-support, or late support payments, are routinely reported to credit bureaus. Under federal law, it turns out, the public agency overseeing court-ordered child-support payments can report a delinquency to a credit bureau once the amount in arrears reaches $1,000.

Therefore, the credit reports and ratings can turn sour on any deadbeat dad or deadbeat mom or any non-custodial parent who just simply fails to earn enough money to meet his/her obligations under court orders.

Nonetheless, if a person promptly, faithfully pays child-support for years, even 18 plus years, that good payment history does not matter to creditors! It is not reported for better credit scoring. It does not help with credit worthiness.

Wouldn't it be fair, just, if you could walk into a mortgage bank and present a report of your excellent history of making child-support payments for 18 years or longer and, at a minimum, be able to obtain credit or better interest rates?

*****

My Judgment:

Understand, I'm not knocking the basic child-support system. It's needed and necessary, often a marvelous tool to support children with absentee fathers. It should, however, be reviewed and revised from time to time. The "one-size-fits-all" principle under which it typically operates can be discriminatory.

*****

Lives have been destroyed, families have been broken, men have been ruined – all with little or no justice, fairness or meaningful child-support delivered!

Would the American Civil Liberties Union help keep you from ruining yourself financially and emotionally if any of the above circumstances were to happen to you?

Probably NOT. The ACLU should take up the cause.

After all, civil liberties have been defined as protection from governmental abuse, and the courts are integral parts of the government. There's little hope for relief in most cases and none whatsoever when the legal action might be construed as being anti-children!

It matters not that the system may be discriminatory at times. You will get little sympathy! The assumption will seem that you must be guilty.

*****

According to my own experience and research, and the legal advice I've received, the cases cited herein, and according to Mr. Robert Franklin's reporting, advice and observations, writing in Our Blog, June 19, 2015, https://nationalparentsorganization.org/blog/22425-new-georgia-law-requires-genetic-testing-in-all-title-iv-d-cases, and in his November 2014 blog – the more common cases with "fathers" who aren't the real fathers go like this:

- A woman gives birth, she receives child-support welfare from the state of residence after naming the father, and the state sends this "father" a notice to show up in court if he wants to "contest paternity."
- This alleged father reads the letter, knows he never met the mom and never had sex with her,

throws the letter away and has no idea that, Mr. Franklin says, "he was signing away 18 years of his income by doing so."

- This purported dad doesn't appear in court, a default judgment is rendered against him, and he gets notice to start paying child-support or reimbursing the state for support that it paid.
- The "dad" who isn't the dad goes to court with DNA test results confirming his claim. But he loses the case, with a *res judicata* decision. He has no legal recourse to fight the decision, and he either starts paying child-support for a child who is not his own or he goes to jail.

Additional warnings, advice and observations offered here also are based on my litigation experience and research, other cases cited herein, and Mr. Franklin's reporting, observations and advice:

- Owing child-support can destroy a deadbeat parent -- man or woman. He or she can be imprisoned or assessed a huge fine. The court can revoke any or all professional licenses and/or ban the man or woman from international travel.

- But anyone, deadbeat or not, who does not respond to any legal notice on child-support or related family matters could face the same destructive results, whether that person is or is not the parent of the child.

- Errors by court employees can further aggravate the outcome, such as entering erroneous names or numbers or dates or any crucial data into court records. Though false, the data could force any accused man or woman, parent or not, into court for hours or days or longer to try to clear up the mistake. A court/government clerk may take the easy path when trying to identify the man or woman being summoned, and the man or woman with the correct name may never get a summons.

- It is easily possible for a man to be declared the father of a child by default, because the man failed to respond to a court summons.

- Many folk summoned by the courts are often confused by the wording therein the summons. They can misunderstand the intent of the summons. Years ago, the legal system ensured better understanding of summons by inserting the words, "You are being sued," into the summons documents.

-   ***If failing to respond to paternity correspondence within 30 days, a man could be declared the father via default!*** So, with a job often taking him out of state or out of the country, for 30 days or longer, a man can become a father by court decision, ordered to pay unaffordable or unreasonable child-support for up to 18 years and perhaps longer and otherwise be legally responsible to father a child or children not his own.

-   A man or woman can be ordered to pay retroactive child-support to the state, with interest. The child-support could be garnished, taken from your wages. Getting your paternity dismissed will be very difficult and expensive – even with DNA proof or the mother swearing that you are not the father, that she does not know you and never seen you before, and that you never had intercourse with her.

-   Citing a report by Diane Dimond, DianeDimond.net, August 31, 2015, and the Women Against Paternity Fraud organization,

Mr. Franklin says in *Our Blog*, September 3, 2015: Paternity fraud "serves no legitimate purpose and harms everyone it touches. When a mother identifies the wrong man as the father of her child, she sets off a ripple of effects that outrage the conscience and potentially threaten lives. . . . Our culture too easily accepts the myth that fathers don't care about or want to help raise their children. Ignoring the true father in a paternity fraud case is part of that false narrative."

Indeed, the system permits a Carnell Alexander of Detroit to get no justice.

Mr. Franklin says Mr. Alexander is a man whom all agree isn't the child's father, but who's required to pay to support (the child) anyway. Yes, the child's mother intentionally lied to child-support enforcement authorities, a fact she now admits. No, the courts never gave Alexander notice of the hearing at which he was adjudicated to be the father. But none of that matters. What matters is that the mother received welfare benefits and the state wants to get repaid. Alexander is the closest thing they have to a dad; so he's the one to pay.

*****

My Judgment:

Mr. Alexander never received official notice of the child-support claim, a requirement in all lawsuits. This in itself should have gotten the suit dismissed.

I agree with Mr. Franklin's declaration that Alexander's case is a true miscarriage of justice on anyone's terms and also about the lessons to be learned from Mr. Alexander's case: Never ever ignore a summon to court. In child-support cases, the state doesn't care if you're the dad or not. What it cares about is getting paid, and any man with money will do. Ignoring the summons in fact makes the state's job easier.

So, guys, never ignore a summons to court. You may spend the next 18 years regretting it.

*****

I recall reading in 2015, in the local paper, about a man whose wife abandoned him and disappeared for years to live as a prostitute and drug addict. He reared their children without her.

After those years, she began attending church and went to court to reclaim custody of the kids. Unbelievably, the court uprooted the children from the man's home and granted full custody to the woman!

He was ordered to pay her child-support.

*****

My Judgment:

I insist that justice was not served, and if that man disagreed with his judge, that man might have angered this judge and been incarcerated. He had a choice of appeal but . . . at a huge financial burden.

*****

In the course of researching and writing about my legal adventures, I met a young athlete named Rob.

The case of Rob seemed typical to me. He was a young man who fathered a child out of wedlock, at a time when neither he nor the child's mother was prepared for parenthood.

Assuming that Rob would be a deadbeat dad, the mother and her mother declared war on him, denying him visits and any time with his son.

The duo's constant demand for child-support payments – on their terms -- drove Rob to pay a visit to the state justice department's child-support division for advice.

Rob was a novice but talented mixed martial arts fighter who was still winning very little money as he dreamt of great fights and, eventually, great paychecks. He

125

was struggling financially when we met. He shared his story with me, and in keeping with the purpose of this book, I advised him to buy the largest box of diapers he could find and a large case of baby formula and take the purchases and $100 in cash with him to pay his son a visit in the stronghold of his avowed foes, the two women.

When he arrived, Rob was met by the baby's mother and her mother outside the home, as if saying by their actions that "you are not welcome here."

At first, they were belligerent, but then Rob pulled out the diapers, baby formula and the cash. Their demeanor changed almost instantly.

To the women's amazement, Rob proceeded to tell them what I recommended that he say: "You know that I don't have much money, and I am struggling."

To the mother of his child, he continued: "But I want you to know that I will be here for you and my son. I bought these (items) to show that I will support the both of you the best I can and will not abandon my son.

"If you need anything, call me and I will see what I can do," Rob emphasized.

After picking their jaws off the ground, both women hugged him and invited him in to see his son. They all chatted for a few hours and played with the child.

A few days later I saw Rob, and he reported that his son's mother and grandmother treated him to dinner out.

Now they all are on good terms. An agreement was reached on his child-support payments and visitation. The child is reaping the benefits that come with money and parental harmony, though without marriage.

*****

My Judgment:

My recommendation to parties in almost any dispute, legal battle or war over a child, his/her care, the parenting rights, custody, visitation, child-support payments or related issues is do what Rob and the two women did, if at all possible:

Talk the issues over, listen to what each other has to say, consult on the possibilities, compromise if at all possible, settle the issues, and come to an agreement – all without involving lawyers and the courts.

Thought of the day for anyone facing prospects of legal action: A bad agreement/settlement is often better than costly litigation even if the legal action is justified by the details/circumstances.

If you have not gotten my message, here it is: Any litigation is costly, in money and far more personal and emotional terms.

*****

I offered an out-of-court arrangement that was similar in all the basics, a fair and reasonable settlement, to my son's mother, and I included $12,000 for a proposed education fund for the child, to make up for any retroactive child-support payments that might be declared in arrears.

Her lawyer rejected the offer, countering with a different, substantially richer deal demanded for her and my son, a deal that I could not afford. I understand that this is a common approach when lawyers are in the mix. In an effort to protect the interests of their clients, lawyers often destroy relationships.

Ours was destroyed!

In the end, combined, my son's mother and I spent nearly $48,000 to fight for our opposing views.

Here's the fiscal result, the bottom line: Our lawyers reaped $48,000 between them. *Our son got $0 for any fund to provide for his future needs!*

Our lawyers could have invested in a BMW/Beemer and a Mercedes. *Our son did not even get a bicycle!*

Our lawyers could have created college tuition savings funds for their kids. *Our son did not get a penny for his forthcoming higher education!*

Our lawyers could afford to buy expensive apparel, hair-styling, manicured nails, etc. *My son's mother went home worn out, beaten, exhausted, with nothing to boost her wardrobe!*

Our lawyers got hefty boosts to their bank accounts. *I went home broke!*

Our boy lost, we lost! . . . on the money and the emotional sides of this legal fight.

But I learned many serious lessons.

I suggested to Rob some things that I learned from several of the attorneys I consulted or hired.

<u>*My Judgment:*</u>

Whenever you hand money to the custodial parent, make the payment by check. Make sure you write on the check that it is "for child-support."

Otherwise, any money paid may be considered a gift to your former lover, and not be counted as child-support.

Believe me, the opposite counsel in a child-support case will have a feast if you do not write that designation.

In my case, all my payments contained that little inclusion on each check.

It helped me win the case!

■ ■

Chapter 6 – A word about dealing with the courts and child- support ...

I was sure the laws were designed to bring the 'ruin' of honorable men.

The first judge/court in my U.S. litigation adventure had – sort of – jurisdiction. *NOT!* That court, in Dallas, could have tried the case if I – the defendant – had allowed the case to move forward there.

There were three primary errors at this early stage of my litigation:

__Error No. 1:__ My former lover's attorney – yes, my former attorney – filed the lawsuit in the wrong jurisdiction. He filed in the wrong County; the case should have been filed in the jurisdiction where I lived. I had to spend money and time to be present and defend myself. The woman, my accuser, was not required to be there however, according to my lawyer. The child-support and paternity case was not heard in Dallas.

*__**Error No. 2:__* Because child's mother never raised any morality issues and never invoked her native country's laws, I was convinced that the second U.S. judge – deemed an "associate judge" in Fort Worth – erred in deciding her court had jurisdiction over child-support issues but not over access, visitation, issues. The decisions came in a jurisdiction hearing, not a trial of the lawsuit filed by that woman in Europe.

***_Error No. 3_, **by this same associate judge:** Though tough-minded and otherwise fair-minded, the associate judge in Fort Worth was ready to decide how much child-support I would be required to pay without deciding whether I could be the father or whether I could have access to my purported child. The DNA test to establish paternity appeared to be an afterthought. I was asked to bring in my tax returns! I was already assumed to be the father and treated as such.

All three errors would cost me money to fix, through no fault of my own. It was my responsibility to bring the mistakes up and pay to have them fixed.

I was flabbergasted, more than once.

Didn't the best interests of the child include frequent and regular visits with his real father? If paternity was established, wouldn't the child reap untold benefits from the influence of a man/father who wanted desperately to be a good father? I was in distress and emotionally

132

broken! Well before paternity was determined, I believed I had a son, but I was denied the right to be a proper father.

*****

My Judgment:

Beware: The legal jargon, concepts, can have some fine, narrow shades of meaning.

Simply put, the associate judge with the correct jurisdiction and the law seemed to be saying: *Who cares if the father – me – ever sees the child or if the father – me – ever plays any other parenting role – whatever! Regardless, that father – me – must provide child-support. I therefore declare the father a human ATM machine.*

*****

During the first hearing in Fort Worth, the same associate judge did NOT bother to inquire about any action to confirm or validate the identity of the mother, the validity of my paternity or the existence or location or condition of the child. Again, I speak as a layman troubled by all the unknowns. The unanswered questions stole my peace.

In the two initial court go-rounds, in Dallas and Fort Worth, the mother and child were not present. Some decisions were being made about a child's future when that

133

child might not exist. The decisions were made on the assumption, not confirmation, that the child existed and that the mother had possession….and that I was a deadbeat dad.

Aside from whether I was the dad or not, the outlook for me was, therefore, to become a human ATM machine for a woman who might not have been who she said she was, who might not have a child, who might not have had possession of the child, who might have abandoned the child or who might have given the child up for adoption. Indeed, the judge did not question whether the child was alive or real, or his whereabouts. NOTE: I assumed, in cases like mine, a clerk of the court could have been directed to research issues or investigate on behalf of the judge. However, no fact-finding took place. Instead, a monetary interest superseded any other matter. The mysterious "Ms. Jane, the mother" was assumed to live around the corner from the court and money would soon be flowing her way. Courts are interesting places, are they not?

Therefore, my hard-earned money could go to satisfy the alleged mother's desires and travels or to her attorney's desires and fraudulent behavior, but not necessarily to support the child, allegedly my son. That was my conclusion, given the circumstances.

Worse yet, had her attorney prevailed in the Dallas (first) go-round of the legal battle, his income from my outgo could have been very lucrative. He had listed his own address as the child's residence. In other words, through intimidating the mother, who knew nothing about American law, he would have received the child-support potentially for his own whims and control. ***The man was a crook!***

Given the initial Dallas court decisions, I was to be nothing more than a source of income for a wealthy lawyer and a woman.

*****

My Judgment, again:

Thus, although she had never paid a penny on a water bill or any taxes in the United States and had not appeared in court or presented the child to me or anyone in this country, this European woman suddenly appeared to have more rights than I did as an American citizen – solely by having a lawyer file suit in a U.S. court! It is that simple and it can be done over and again. In the United States, anyone – regardless of country of origin – can have her/his day in court for

135

**almost any reason. Fairness and justice may
not be served.**

"Yo dije, maldita sea la justicia" – translated, *"I
said, damn justice!"*

*****

Fortunately for me, a great many judges in lower courts are
believed to be making errors of judgment. Appeals are
rather common. Even the family courts of appeal are open
8 a.m. to 5 p.m. on workdays.

So, let's start the detailed explanation of my case
back at Error No.1, the matter of jurisdiction: Normally in
the United States a mother suing for child-support will file
her case in the county of the child's or children's residence
or in her own county of residence or in the county of
residence of the party being sued. Neither my former lover
nor her/our child born out of wedlock had ever lived in the
United States; so, the next logical choice for filing would
have been my county of residence. *So, what a surprise?*
The mother's attorney filed suit in a family court in Dallas
County.

As it turned out, the law stipulated that the suit for
child-support (or any civil lawsuit, as a matter of fact) be
filed in my county of residence. Tarrant County was the

county with proper jurisdiction to decide this issue focused on me.

Nonetheless, I was still expected to pay my attorney, unplanned and unnecessary expense, to take action to have the case transferred to my county of residence. The family courts, in other words, did not resolve this "mistake" made by the lawyer for my adversary. And, I discovered, it's not the court's job to do so.

So, why Dallas, anyway? That shyster for the mother filed in the county of his U.S. office location – for his convenience. The court was an easy walk from his workplace. My options were to drive the two-hour roundtrip to be in court to defend myself or to pay my attorney to correct the venue. I had to take time off work, drive to Dallas, appear in court and spend more money.

In my situation, there were a couple of additional twists.

Here's a clarification of the legal standing for venue: According to the Texas Legal Code, the law normally requires that a child-support lawsuit be filed in the child's or children's state of residence and in the child's county of residence. Since the mother and child lived overseas, the Uniform Parentage Act – a law that has been amended and passed by the State of Texas and several other states – was applicable to our situation: If neither the child nor the mother lives or has ever lived in the United States while any other party to the suit resides in a state, the jurisdiction goes to that state and county of residence for that U.S. resident. In this case, an international court had no jurisdiction.

That also means the case was incorrectly filed in Dallas County.

Here were the twists: Before my attorney could follow through on the filing to change the venue, *thank God*, my case was dismissed by the Dallas County court. Yet, I had almost coughed up an additional $2,800 for my lawyer, including $1,500 to cover what would have become largely unnecessary work toward the transfer. After all, my lawyer would have invested time and effort; that would be no fault of hers. But my case dismissal saved me that $2,800. Well, no need to pity my attorney. She didn't walk away empty-handed; I had paid her a $2,500 retainer, which she took with her and exited my legal adventure.

And she was my fourth U.S. attorney!

The first was the shyster turned adversary; the second and third were paid for consultations only as I educated myself on family law matters.

You see, I figured I would be dealing with international law, and in my desire to land the best attorney, I relied initially on the first seven of the overall nine lawyers, most being mistaken in their advice. The first seven were highly qualified in family law but knew very little, next to nothing, about international treaties and litigation dealing with international child-support. To save money, I invested thousands of hours researching the subject and presented my findings to each of the lawyers.

Later with No. 8 of the nine lawyers, I appealed, arguing that my assumptions were correct, that Errors 2 and 3 were indeed legal miscalculations, as I pursued access to the boy that I wanted to be my biological son and to be my son in an actual father-son relationship.

Lawyer No. 8 was a very sharp, independent lawyer who practiced exclusively in my county. Hiring her gave me a tactical advantage as no doubt she would be known and respected by the judges with whom she frequently worked. She represented me on that short appeal to the Senior Judge, and then I hired her for my trial, which we won.

Lawyer number 9 was my appeal lawyer, and last attorney, the one who represented me in the mother's appeal.

My Judgment:

Lessons learned: A judge typically does not act as a teacher of the law in court and will not put up with a lawyer's incompetence, ignorance of the law and or lack of preparation. A court is not law school.

At this early stage in the process, I wish the judge had met privately with both parties to the suit and their lawyers prior to the first public hearing – to hear the merits of the case from both sides. That did not happen, making it difficult for the case to proceed on the real issues.

But the courts will fit you in, and it will cost you!

*****

Remember, no one knew – at that time – whether this child was mine, other than the mother. Still, the legal bills kept coming! Had the DNA results shown the child was not mine, my money would be gone forever.

Meanwhile, because I lived in Texas and the Uniform Parentage Act was applicable, the case came under the jurisdiction of a Tarrant County family court. The so-called *Personam* -- *"my person is here"* -- principle

140

was applied, giving said jurisdiction to a local court in my own county of residence. In other words, the local court had me and that was enough to proceed. I was fortunate, I think, that my first judge in Dallas County was a woman, handling the first substantial hearing. This judge mostly, proved to be fair, firm and unwilling to put up with any nonsense, and she taught the shyster attorney that her court was no law school.

I was even more fortunate to have a great job with a reputable petroleum company. I served as corporate manager for the company's "Environmental, Health and Safety Affairs" branch, at the executive level. Accordingly, I had a healthy salary with hefty benefits. Nonetheless, nearly two-thirds of my paycheck was going to lawyers. And this was just the beginning of my litigation adventures.

On the positive side, as a corporate executive, I had a great boss and a flexible schedule that allowed me to move around and dictate my own daily activities. It did help that the venue for my case was moved to a court in Fort Worth, just a few blocks from my office; showing up in court was no inconvenience. I got the convenience denied to that shyster.

I was well-heeled, as they say, but not rich, and I certainly was going to appeal the associate judge's decisions during my Tarrant first round of child-support litigation in Fort Worth. I was ready to fight, regardless of the cost.

Let's be clear about my situation, with a review:

I thought I was going to be ordered to pay an as-yet-undetermined sum of child-support before I had been declared the legitimate, legal, scientifically proven father of the child born in Europe. Of course, eventually, I was wrong on this assumption; but it certainly stole my sleep.

In Fort Worth, after the venue change, the associate judge denied jurisdiction for taking any action on my pursuit of visitation, father parenting time, with my alleged child.

I had previously been paying child-support even though no court order existed for that purpose. In court, I held in my hand a mound of receipts for payments I had made. Nothing of this, however, was mentioned to the associate judge in my case. The judge didn't consider it either. To her, I might simply have been another deadbeat alcoholic, drug-addict, criminal father, woman beater and child abuser not paying child-support. Such people are the court's more typical clientele.

I had not committed any crime. I simply had intimate relations with a woman later claiming to be the mother of my child. I knew that DNA testing was ahead, probably at the appeals level.

I had already discovered, after consulting with my attorneys, that any woman from anywhere in the world can claim to have a baby by any man. Any lawyer can sue you on behalf of any woman in the world. That baby and/or that woman may not exist or may no longer be alive. This can happen repeatedly, and the court will provide a forum for discovering of facts ... at your expense.

Soon I was to learn that a court can order anyone to submit to DNA testing, and the accused will need to spend, never to recoup, money on the testing costs, attorneys and other legal fees.

If you cannot afford an attorney, in a child support suit, you are on your own, and the court will NOT assign you a lawyer. Should you not be able to defend yourself by representing yourself or if you do not appear in court at all, you will lose by default, and if you don't pay the court-ordered child-support, you'll probably be incarcerated. It's that simple!

I was astounded by the thought that, had a court clerk made an error as often happens, I could have gone to jail. Out of curiosity, I conducted a search online for this: "court clerk error lands man in jail." I was amazed at the number of cases where people have either been wrongly incarcerated or wrongly freed as the result of a court clerk's error.

I was in a frenzy of trying to anticipate all the possibilities in the court proceedings and decisions.

I learned that should it be found through DNA testing that you are not the father, the court will likely NOT allow you to recover damages or have previous child-support payments returned to you. Recouping money is not allowed under the Tex. Fam. Code Ann.§ 160.316 (f). It doesn't matter if you never met the woman. You cannot sue her to get your legal fees even if you can prove the whole thing was a hoax, a fraud, a scam! And if you should seek a review of your child-support payment rate and get a reduction months later after filing for the review, there likely will be no way to get a retroactive reduction dating to the date of filing for the review.

The judge will not order a recipient parent to return money you spent on your legal defense against knowingly false accusations and will not order said parent to return already-paid funds despite any reduction in support pay rate.

Well, in my case, the mother lives in a foreign country, and the local Texas court has no practical, actionable authority over her.

A Texas court may not bother to validate the existence of the child or mother it would however bother to incarcerate you very quickly.

It may not matter to the court whether the woman is who she claims to be, whether the child exists or not, whether you are actually the father, whether the alleged mother's claims have any merit – unless you hire an attorney to challenge the identity of the woman, the existence of the child, your paternity of the child or the validity of the claims. If not, the judgment will stand, and you will owe the money!

The onus of providing proof falls on the defendant. It fell on me.

Let's examine an example, a true case involving a friend. It's an extraordinary case.

As a young man, college student, my friend dated a young woman who eventually got pregnant and claimed the child was his. He did not challenge her claim and believed the boy was his biological son. He then decided to establish a permanent relationship with the woman, and they moved in together.

The relationship did not last as he uncovered that she was being unfaithful. Eventually, they went separate ways, and he moved from his native country to the United States, started a new life and remarried. He worked for a large American corporation for 33 years as a robotics engineer and finally retired.

A few years ago, my friend confided in me that his assumed son, then 42 years old, asked if my friend would sponsor him and his family coming to the United States so that he could obtain a green card and they could obtain citizenship. Well, his assumed son had reason to expect the help; after all, my friend had sent child-support payments to this man's mother and then later adult-support payments to this man.

My friend, meanwhile, had established a new family. As a 33-year veteran engineer with a reputable company, he had accumulated assets. Speaking to the assumed son, my friend voiced a desire to ensure financial security for his U.S. family after his own death. Upon his demise, he didn't want the man and his family to bring any legal issues or challenges. So, in order to protect his U.S. family, my friend wanted to get a DNA test done.

The test results revealed that the assumed son was not his biological son!

My friend had provided nearly 40 years of financial support to this man not knowing that he was not his child.

Knowing what I learned about family courts and state child-support enforcement divisions, it's safe to say that my friend had a "son" overseas even if they did not share any genes.

DNA is a wonderful tool, and it is highly recommended that, when in doubt and maybe not, a test be conducted.

The DNA test for me was forthcoming, as my adventure continued – with more drama in the courtroom and post-trial, as well.

To this point in my narrative, as you've read, I have not covered my entire legal case, and my personal story also remains incomplete. I provide the following overview summary – of my personal story and legal timeline, from start to finish – to serve as a guide, with some additional details:

My story/case so far:

- In 2003, I was informed that I was the father of a child soon to be born to a woman, a native of Eastern Europe, with whom I had a love affair.

- I started making child-support and additional support payments under my own initiative, at $500 and often more per month.
- I ran into employment and financial difficulties and had to reduce my rate to $300 a month, still a substantial amount of money in Eastern Europe at that time. But the mother wanted more money, and she soon broke off communications with me, and disappeared from my own radar.
- In 2005, I contacted a representative from my son's country and also a dual European/American lawyer who resided in Dallas, to locate the baby boy whom I believed I had fathered but whose whereabouts I had lost track of. At the time, without a court order or other legal mandate, I had been paying child support for more than two years.
- I considered the European lawyer to be my attorney in an anticipated lawsuit for visitation, to be filed against my former lover. But he contacted her, the mother, and signed her as his client.

<u>My story/case continuing</u> … yours, as well, might have no end:

- I received a notice from the Texas State Attorney General's Office Child Support Division, saying that I owed child-support. The shyster lawyer had reported me as a "deadbeat dad" to the state authorities. I voluntarily met with an Attorney General's representative and showed them receipts of payments for child support; no child-support orders were issued by the state.

- The European lawyer then filed a child-support lawsuit in a Dallas family court, but the case was dismissed. Jurisdiction, paternity and other legalities remained unsettled issues.

  And I still had received no word about my boy or his whereabouts.

Victory for me! Temporarily!

- I expected another lawsuit was forthcoming; so I began my long-distance contacts with lawyers in Europe and my research into European, international and other family law.

- The mother secured another attorney, and this time the case was filed in the county family

149

court that had proper jurisdiction – Tarrant County, where I lived. I hired my eighth attorney.

- An associate judge, a woman, in this local family court in Fort Worth heard the allegations. Mother and child had not yet appeared in court or for any related legal matter.

- Still not having met or seen the mother and/or child, the associate judge ruled initially that her court had jurisdiction for the lawsuit, that I had to pay some level of child-support and that her court did not have jurisdiction over deciding whether I should have visitation rights with the child alleged to be my son. The same judge did not address the paternity issue.

I lost this round!

- I appealed the preliminary decisions of the associate judge to a senior judge.

- The appeal brought the case to trial in 2009, before the senior judge in the local family court system in Fort Worth, Texas. The mother appeared in court for the first time.

- The senior judge, a man, ordered DNA tests for me and the baby.

I am the father!

- Once my paternity was established, the senior
  judge granted me visitation rights and ordered
  me to pay a reduced, less than half the amount,
  monthly rate for child-support. But he also ruled
  out any obligation for me to pay retroactive
  child-support, a nearly $60,000 amount.

- Additionally, the judge's decision added that,
  until the child was old   enough, the mother was
  to purchase her own ticket and half the child's
  ticket (father would pay the other half) and
  bring the child to the United States for
  visitation. During Christmas, she was to pay the
  entire ticket for the child to travel to be with me
  in Texas.

I won this one, a huge one! I got my parental visits and
finally get to be with my boy. *This was a victory in a pro-
woman, pro-mother court, a huge one!*

- The mother appealed the senior judge's
  decisions, specifically the child-support rate, the
  order to pay for travel and the rejection of
  retroactive child-support payments.

- In the 2009 hearing before the final appeals
  court for family law, the three-judge panel

upheld all aspects of the senior judge's decisions. The mother lost on nearly every issue argued during the litigation. She gained court-ordered child-support at a rate that I could afford to pay. And I wanted to support my son.

They lost big!

- In the end, we – the mother, our son and I – all lost big, in terms of money immediately and for investment in our son's future, time together with our son, parenting time for me, our own emotional wellbeing and the solid goodwill that could have been built between the mother and me!

There would be need for healing time ahead.

*****

My Judgment:

As my pal lawyer said, "A bad agreement is better than a good litigation."

If you are able, stay away from the courts and do your part; for me, it had been a long but not good ride in spite of the victories.

Rather, a compromise is better. You will not get everything you want, no matter

how you pursue your goals. That's the courts!

Wish you well on your journey!

Chapter 7 – *The history of child-support surprised me.*

I really did believe prior to my litigation, and still believe, that our legal framework for establishing and requiring and enforcing child-support is a wonderful effort to care for children. Just NOT perfect. It's not always on the fairness/justice path.

I like the quote from Reinhold Niebuhr, the American Theologian and intellectual, who said:

> *"Man's capacity for justice makes democracy possible; but man's inclination to injustice makes democracy necessary."*

Many recent laws, law amendments and related developments on child-support and child well-being have been implemented across many of our states.

One interesting view by a judge deals with adoption and abandonment of a child. On the Hispanic television network show *Caso Cerrado (Closed Case)*, produced by Telemundo, Judge Ana Maria Polo had her own child-support view during a child-custody case: Whenever a parent decides to give up a child to state custody for the purpose of the child being adopted, the judge said, that parent must then pay child-support to the state. In other words, the state becomes the child caretaker, and the former parent now owes the state. *Even though he/she is no longer the parent.*

Over the centuries before there was a legal framework for child-support standards and enforcement, man – and I do mean *"MAN"* – was more than inclined to injustice when it came to providing – or not providing – the minimum of funds or provisions for the nurturing or just for the survival of offspring born out of wedlock or residing with a divorced mother or otherwise cast-off wife or cast-out concubine.

Outlining that long history prior to any serious child-support enforcement and describing how women of earlier U.S. generations cared for their children as they ventured to work, Dr. Sonya Michel, history professor at the University of Maryland, wrote:

"American mothers have invented many ways to care for their children while they work.

Native Americans strapped newborns to cradle boards or carried them in woven slings;

Colonial women placed small children on standing stools... to prevent them from falling into the fireplace.

Pioneers on the Midwestern plains laid infants in wooden boxes fastened to the beams of their plows.

155

Southern dirt farmers tethered their runabouts to pegs driven into the soil at the edge of their fields.

White southern planters' wives watched African-American boys and girls playing in the kitchen yard while their mothers toiled in the cotton fields.

African-American mothers sang white babies to sleep while their own little ones comforted themselves.

Migrant laborers shaded infants in baby tents set in the midst of beet fields.

Cannery workers put children to work beside them stringing beans and shelling peas.

Shellfish processors sent toddlers to play on the docks, warning them not to go near the water."

(Michel, S. (2011). The history of child care in the U.S. Retrieved, January 23, 2016 from http://www.socialwelfarehistory.com/programs/child-care-the-american-history/) (Note: with apologies to Dr. Michel for our paragraphing modifications.)

In the early 19th Century, the Website http://www.child-support-laws-state-by-state.com reports, American courts found that the laws of that era did not provide for action on child-support claims when dealing with divorce cases or other marital failures.

American laws were little different than English laws of the time. Under these laws, a father could not be required, forced or ordered to support his children under almost any circumstances, the Website reports. One clear exception was when such support had been agreed to, or pre-authorized, by a contract with the said father.

Another law allowed "limited recovery." Under a law called the Elizabethan Poor Law of 1601, a local parish could recover some child-support funds to be spent for the care of a single mother and her children not otherwise supported by the children's father. But the circumstances which activated that recovery were harsh: the mother and children had to be totally impoverished. And "any third parties or single mothers could not directly ask for reimbursement of support expenses," according to the Website.

Ah, but this impoverished area of law didn't stop good old American determination, modification, legislation and codification.

American courts began to find ways to declare "that a father had a legal obligation to support his offspring," the Website states.

In one of the earliest of these cases favoring support, Stanton vs. Wilson in 1808, the courts were dealing with a child-abuse situation. The Supreme Court of Connecticut declared that Eunice Stanton could recover child-support "from her first husband on behalf of her deceased second husband . . ." The first husband, her ex-spouse, was the father of her children, and she had been awarded custody of two of her three children because the father had been abusive to the children. Fearing abuse, the third one had fled from his father.

But what was most important for laws to come, "the court clearly stated in this case that the children's father was legally bound 'to protect, educate, and maintain their legitimate children.' Similar cases in New York and New Jersey asserted that a father could be held financially responsible for the welfare of his children," according to http://www.child-support-laws-state-by-state.com.

As U.S. case law developed in the child-support area, after the 1850s, a two-part test evolved in the courts, the Website stated, as follows:

1. Were the support items provided by the plaintiff, the mother, "bare subsistence" necessities, such as food and clothing?

2. Had the father been "negligent in providing those items himself?"

But as the courts began to side more with the mothers, the courts also continued to require divorced women "to show proof that their spouse was at fault for the divorce."

And typically, "the father was only obligated to pay support for the bare maintenance of the child. By the late nineteenth century, almost every state in the nation had on its books some legally enforceable duty for a father to support his children," according to http://www.child-support-laws-state-by-state.com.

As reported on another website, http://singleparents.about.com/od/paternity/a/history-of-child-support.htm, "the United States government began legislating child support enforcement more than 100 years ago." Here's a partial timeline of key legal decisions in the 20th Century, as outlined on the website:

In 1910, the Uniform Desertion and Non-Support Act was adopted by the National Conference of Commissions on Uniform State Laws. Covering only 24 jurisdictions, this law "made it a crime for a husband to willfully abandon or neglect to provide support for children under the age of 16." But the law did not provide sufficient enforcement teeth. Parents leaving the covered jurisdiction often escaped having to pay child-support.

The year 1950 was a major turning point in child-support law.

In 1950, the Social Security Act Amendment 42 U.S.C. § 602(a)(11) enabled the federal government to require "state welfare agencies to notify law enforcement officials when providing Aid to Families with Dependent Children (AFDC)." The program would become the so-called "welfare" and is now labeled as Temporary Assistance to Needy Families (TANF). The stated purpose of the law was to require parents to be responsible for providing for their children, "in an effort to relieve the state – and the taxpayers – of that responsibility. To this day, custodial parents applying for government assistance are required to provide information about the location of the other parent for this purpose," according to singleparents.about.com/od/paternity/a/history-of-child-support.htm.

In 1950 also came the Uniform Reciprocal Enforcement of Support Act (URESA), approved by the National Conference of Commissioners on Uniform State Laws and the American Bar Association, allowing states to pursue parents across state lines for the collection of child-support and for enforcing other legally required responsibilities to their children.

Federal laws and amendments and related legal decisions began to multiply for an evolving child-support system, including acts and decisions in 1965, 1967, 1974, 1976 and 1981. The 1974 measure, a Social Security Act amendment, strengthened states' efforts to collect child-support. Federal funding for states became more important where child-support enforcement was involved, according to the about.com Website.

In 1981, deadbeat dads became targets of the Internal Revenue Service. The Omnibus Budget Reconciliation Act of 1981 "authorized the Internal Revenue Service to withhold federal income tax refunds in cases where the recipient is delinquent in paying court-ordered child support. The same amendment allows states to withhold a portion of unemployment benefits for the same purpose and prevents child-support payments from being discharged in bankruptcy proceedings," about.com reports.

The Family Support Act of 1988 (P.L. 100-485) "allows states to garnish wages for the purpose of collecting child-support and requires states to maintain clearly defined child-support guidelines."

The Child Support Recovery Act of 1992 (P.L. 102-521) "allows states to prosecute parents who willfully choose not to pay child-support."

The Personal Responsibility and Work Opportunity Reconciliations Act of 1996 (PRWORA), among other related provisions boosting governments' powers to track child-support violators, "streamlined the process for establishing paternity, allowing biological fathers to voluntarily acknowledge paternity."

The Deadbeat Parents Punishment Act (DPPA) "increased the consequences for parents who willfully choose not to pay child support." Fines can be increased up to $10,000, and parents failing to pay child-support for a child in another state can face up to two years in prison, about.com reports.

Thus, the history of collecting child-support began with citizens taking in destitute mothers and the poor and then trying to get family members or fathers to pitch in financially to support the mothers and children. The states long ago began implementing their own various laws and systems for handling child-support issues; state laws evolved and improved for decades. But then began the still ongoing federalization of child-support requirements.

A good article on this federalization – "Collecting Child Support: A History of Federal and State Initiatives," by Naomi Cahn and Jane C. Murphy, located at http://scholarship.law.gwu.edu/faculty_publications – can be found on the George Washington University Law School's Website: www.ncahn@law.gwu.edu It's part of the GW Law Faculty Publications & Other Works Faculty

Scholarship 2000. Cahn was identified as a professor of law at George Washington University Law School; Murphy, a professor of law and director of clinical programs at the University of Baltimore School of Law, at the time the articles were published in 2000.

Now it's accurate to say that for more than 40 years, the federal role in the child-support area has been expanding. The growing role affects state management of state child-support programs and enforcement.

The Cahn/Murphy article states:

"Although the federal government had become involved in child-support programs much earlier, the Social Security amendments of 1974 signaled the beginning of the contemporary federal-state partnership approach to child support. Through this legislation, Congress mandated the creation of the federal Office of Child Support Enforcement and required that states participate in various programs of that office to increase the effectiveness of child-support collections. Congress adopted the 1974 amendments in an effort to remedy a steadily increasing number of female-headed households living in poverty, which it blamed on the rising number of absent fathers."

The article cited U.S. Senate Finance Committee reports showing that "that from 1959 to 1968, while the poverty rate 'for male-headed families went down to 7 percent, poverty among female-headed families increased to 32 percent,' rising even further to 36 percent by 1970."

The article continued:

"Before the adoption of child-support guidelines in the late 1980s, judges relied on broad discretionary standards to decide how much a noncustodial parent must pay in child-support. These vague standards were applied in any case in which child-support was established, including in divorce, separation or paternity proceedings in which initial support was set, or in modification proceedings. Traditionally most states' statutes simply instructed the court that 'parents had an obligation to support their child.' Case law interpreting these statutory provisions required courts, when setting the amount of support, to consider the needs of the child and the noncustodial spouse's ability to pay."

But in practice, the article stipulated, the considerations led to inconsistencies: "An utter lack of uniformity not only between states but also within states characterized the setting of the level of child-support.

"Against the background of these failed efforts . . .
since 1974 the federal government has become increasingly
involved in state child-support efforts and now requires
child-support guidelines, wage withholding, the registering
of new hires, and other methods to improve child-support
collection."

When the United States implemented child-support
laws, the laws were and are still intended to prevent parents
from relying on the state for financial support for their
children.

Congress punctuated this maneuver, starting with
the passage of the Family Support Act, Title IV-D of the
Social Security Act, in 1974, which applied to states
receiving federal funds: Those states must establish and
enforce parental child-support obligations.

In her book **Child Support Guidelines:**
Interpretation and Application, Laura W. Morgan
explains that at some point, child-support amounts were left
to the discretion of the judge. That has changed. Now
states have a guide that must be followed by the courts in
awarding child-support. Some states follow a combination
of both parents' incomes while others consider only the
income of the non-custodial parent, the one who has to pay.
In Texas for example, the guide states that the obligor to

pay child-support must pay 20 percent of his/her after-tax wages for one child, with 5 percent increments for each child thereafter. For more on this guide, see the following link: http://www.ncsl.org/research/human-services/guideline-models-by-state.aspx

In my unusual situation, the judge reduced the amount of child-support, deviating from the standard or norm, by more than fifty percent- I otherwise would have had to pay substantially.

The mother's lawyer saw that decision by the judge as an opportunity to set up a hearing, seeking to have the judge's rendition reversed. The judge, however, once again sustained the original decision. That's when the mother appealed. Eventually, the judge simply put in writing the reasoning behind his original decision, and that was the end of it. All the money and time spent on the appeal was a waste.

How a court handles any decision on child-support rates is becoming more predictable and federal action is the key reason.

Congress enacted the Child Support Enforcement Amendments Act in 1984, requiring the states to toughen their child-support and related laws and to strengthen their enforcement powers related to child-support.

This is how you could be affected: Under the act, states must require employers to withhold child-support from paychecks of parents who are delinquent on payments by one month or longer; provide for the imposition of liens against the property of anyone defaulting on child-support obligations; and deduct from federal and state income tax refunds all unpaid child-support obligations.

Meanwhile, in recent years, one of the most significant changes in child-support enforcement policy has been the shift towards addressing men's roles as fathers.

For example, the Personal Responsibility and Work Opportunity Reconciliation Act revises child-support legislation to call for the development of a number of social services programs to work with fathers. It has been a huge positive step.

Under this act, as applied to my case, that associate judge who ruled that I should be an ATM machine -- whether I had a relationship with my child or not -- was wrong.

The laws for child-support are designed with the goal of having the best interests of the child in mind -- though in some court decisions that directive has come up short. I cited earlier, for example, the case of a woman who abandoned her husband and children and, for 12 years, lived a life as a drug addict and prostitute. One day she found religion and went to court to gain custody of her children. To everyone's amazement, the judge ordered the children to be taken away from the father who had taken care of them all those years, granted her custody, and ordered him to pay her child-support. *By the way, the judge never ordered her to pay him retroactive child-support for the 12 years she failed to pay him! She owed him!*

So, what is fair or unfair when deciding who pays and how much?

*****

My Judgment:

If one parent enjoys a higher than subsistence-level standard of living, the child should be entitled to share in the benefit of that improved standard.

During my case, I pondered, what about a woman living in one of the poorest parts of the world and has a child by an American man?

Let's assume the man earns $50,000.00 a year and the mother's yearly income is a mere $400. In many states, the woman is set to receive 20 percent of his income (after taxes); that is nearly $10,000 a year. In her part of the world, she would live in wealth as an elite member of society, and the child, assuming she spends the money on him, would be set for life. While she will live in wealth in her country, the American on the other hand, will just live a middle-class lifestyle. This area of the current law needs revisiting.

Sure in this hypothetical situation, the father is well-heeled and the child should also live well. I agree. But I am suggesting that adjustments must be made to be more equitable. One parent should not suffer while the other is enriched.

*****

On the National Conference of State Legislatures Website, www.ncsl.org, April 2013, the article titled "Child Support Guidelines Model" details a unique form of calculating the amount of child-support to be paid. It uses a formula called the **Melson Formula**. This formula incorporates several public policy judgments designed to ensure that each parent's basic needs are met in addition to the children's. The formula was designed to consider income from both parents and accordingly, ensure parents are not driven to ruin over child-support responsibility. Under this formula, as it was my case, both parents are required to submit and report accurate data on income and assets.

Still not in general or wide use across the nation, the Melson Formula was developed by a Delaware Family Court judge and fully explained in Dalton v. Clanton, 559 A.2d 1197 (Del. 1989). As of this writing however, only three states (Delaware, Hawaii and Montana) use the Melson Formula.

As many non-custodial parents struggle to keep financially afloat themselves while paying child-support, this formula is not a bad idea. What if the economy tanks and jobs are scarce and the parents are unable to find or hold jobs long enough to pay their debts and their already mandated child-support at levels determined when economic times were flush?

One helpful resource for a child-support model is the National Conference of State Legislatures (http://www.ncsl.org/research/human-services/guideline-models-by-state.aspx). As noted on the conference's Website, Texas uses the "Percentage of Obligor's" Income, usually the father's income, to determine child-support levels. But most states use a formula that incorporates shares of income of both parents.

I like the latter. Don't you?

I have a friend who made good money in a business he started. He and his wife divorced and she remarried a very wealthy business man. The court has failed to consider the fact that she is wealthy, and my friend pays child-support as if her income does not matter.

Researching and understanding the history of child-support provided answers to many of my questions. *But there are far too many questions of fairness still to be answered.*

I am now a part of that history, as well!

Chapter 8 – *Let's fight the law ... The Trial!*

I was a bag of sweat, shaking, nervous, weary.

THE TRIAL was, for all serious and pertinent reasons and issues, my *fourth round* in the courtroom.

The first round was a hearing in a Dallas County family court where my child-support case was dismissed. A shyster lawyer submitted to the court unacceptable documentation, and for that reason, the judge dismissed the case. I was ready to seek a transfer to a Tarrant County family court. The case had been filed by the attorney for the mother of my child, but it was filed in the wrong jurisdiction, the correct jurisdiction being the Fort Worth area/Tarrant County where I resided. I didn't have to pursue the transfer because of the dismissal. That saved me at least $2,800. The first round amounted to a draw for both parties.

The second round was a hearing stemming from the refiling of the child-support lawsuit, filed this time by a new, top-dollar attorney for the mother, and this time filed

172

in the proper jurisdiction, a Tarrant County family law court in Fort Worth.

In this second hearing, an associate judge made two limited decisions – one declaring that the court had jurisdiction over determining the level of child-support I should have to pay and the other decision declaring that the court had no jurisdiction over whether I should be given custody and/or visitation rights to enable me to be, at least, a good long-distance father to my son living in Eastern Europe. This hearing was also noted for its lack of specific orders, decisions or determinations: No decision was rendered on the child-support rate to be paid; no decision was rendered on whether I was, in fact, the father of the child; and no determinations were made to confirm the existence of the child, the caregiver for the child and/or the whereabouts of the child; the mother did not appear in court. And the court refused to consider the issue of custody and/or visitation rights for me. Indeed, I lost the second round.

How these details and other key decisions were to be made remained a mystery to me, and I decided to appeal the no-jurisdiction decision on my pursuit of custody and/or visitation rights.

In this third round, my appeal to the senior judge of the Tarrant County family courts was the move that translated into *The Trial*, the one that proved to be crucial in this legal adventure of mine. In a very real sense, the first three rounds/hearings amounted to preliminaries.

That third round was the brief, informal but official hearing with both lawyers meeting before the senior judge in the same trial court where the jurisdiction issues arose. But the judge this time was a man, the senior trial judge.

This hearing was a "Yes-or-No" matter with the judge agreeing that *The Trial* would deal with child-support, visitation/custody and all related matters. But first, the judge wanted to clear the record by establishing certainty of paternity. The short, pre-trial appeal hearing resulted in the judge ordering the DNA testing.

Once that was settled, that I was indeed the father, *The Trial* was scheduled to begin, and I was that bag of sweat, shaking, nervous, weary. I slept little the night before.

Throughout the day, on the day before *The Trial,* I wrote an outline of what I could answer on some of the anticipated forthcoming questions. I was going to be ready for the fourth round.

On my kitchen counter, near to my car keys, I placed documents that included the stack of receipts for all my payments to the mother, the instructions from my lawyer and, yes, the address to the courthouse. It's critical to arrive for court on time. With the vagaries of rampant road construction in many areas and traffic snarls, it's better leave your house with ample time to spare. Do you have change or an ATM/debit/credit card for the parking meter? How far is the parking from the courthouse? Finding convenient free parking is tough, and if it's a mile or more to walk to court, in Texas heat, you'd want to dress in shorts and sneakers – not attire recommended for court.

The night before the court hearing, I set out my clothes, shined my shoes and laid out a nice tie. All I had to do on the morning of trial: shave, take a nice warm shower, dress and then groom.

I walked up a long flight of steps, dozens of steps, and wondered if court buildings were purposely built with long steep stairs to enable litigants to relieve stress before they finish climbing. Maybe a stupid idea? But it worked for me.

I was a lonely man ready to stand in the arena of gladiators. I arrived in court with time to spare, sat

175

peacefully next to my lawyer and tried to calm down. Not an easy thing to do. The stair climb helped.

I wore a nicely pressed, long-sleeved dress shirt and a neck tie. I wanted to show respect for the court. Marking her first U.S. court appearance, the mother was also already there, in the courtroom. She wore very simple clothing, no jewelry, nothing pricey. It's a family lawyers' tactic: Give the appearance of being needy on the financial front, or at least not well-heeled. *Here's that rich guy and then here's this poor, maybe destitute, certainly needy and deserving woman.*

There were no bands playing outside or inside. No TV cameras purring. No flashing cameras. No throngs of reporters. Not even one news reporter. Not surprising. Most court decisions – even many that affect the destiny of a society -- are made by a handful of people in a small courtroom. My trial would not change any society's destiny. It could very well change my own. It was critical to my future.

Only seven people were in the courtroom: the judge, a bailiff, the court clerk taking notes, the two lawyers, the mother and me. We litigants with our attorneys sat at two tables. On the left side of the main entrance, for those walking in, I sat next to my lawyer. The mother and her attorney sat on the right side. The room was small and seemed crowded despite the lack of a crowd.

My attorney was a solo practicing lawyer with a small office in an old, low-rent office complex. She was a woman standing more than 6 feet tall, very articulate and evincing a relaxed demeanor. Her easy-going manner, however, sparked concerns for me. I thought she was too nice, too sweet or too unconcerned and too easy on the opposition at times, certainly way too cordial with the adversarial counsel.

She was very respectful of the court, solidly professional. A lawyer friend of mine later commented, "She's a very good lawyer!"

I came to describe her as a calm but powerful river that runs very deep, dragging everything in its path. Due to her size and calm demeanor, she was an intimidating presence. My lawyer limited her practice territory exclusively to my county of residence; this was an advantage. With such limited service area, she routinely dealt with the same lawyers and the same courts, and she knew them all well.

Then there was the mother's attorney, a top-dollar lawyer from a prominent law firm in Dallas. Due to heavy traffic, she drove two hours to fight me, at last, in this one major legal battle in my county and near my office.

In many ways very much the opposite of my lawyer, she was a gray-haired woman, a diminutive, fast-paced, who walked swinging from side to side into the courtroom, almost on the tips of her toes. I thought, "Boy, she appeared in a hurry!" She stayed in a hurry during the entire trial, it seemed to me. This older lawyer reminded me of an old librarian looking hurriedly for books and talking fast, rolling out long streams of sentences.

But her appearance could fool you. She was a formidable cross-examiner and a good lawyer, mostly.

Then, a middle-aged male judge walked in, and **The Trial** began.

"I will open this procedure warning the lawyers that I will treat this case as if the mother and child live in Fort Worth. Mother has submitted herself and the child to the jurisdiction of this court, and I will treat her as such. I don't want any excuses for her not to appear in court, and I don't want distance to be used as an impediment," the judge declared.

I recalled that the old savvy lawyer I consulted early on in Dallas had mentioned that the mother's lawyer made

178

a mistake by placing her client under the authority of Texas courts.

But then again, the mother had to go before Texas judges if she wanted to get any child-support declared legally and any court order to require payment.

The graying, opposing counsel was given the nod to start the proceeding, and she asked to question me. I was asked to take a seat in the witness chair, a nondescript, ugly gray thing that even looked uncomfortable.

I was about to encounter my first big surprise in court.

It started months before while the mother visited in Texas and when we were still on cordial footing. She, the child and I took a mini-vacation together, and we took pictures. Little did I know that those pictures had a hidden purpose. They showed up in court and were presented, to prove paternity.

In those photos, I held the boy in my arms, played and fed him. The child and I swam with dolphins and fed animals at the zoo, all shown well in the photos.

On the positive side, the images presented the good side of me, taking care of my son. Those were our good old days!

In a flash, the mother's attorney turned from cordial and friendly to aggressive in her questioning. She wanted to establish clear paternity and used the photos and trips to show a relationship between father and son.

But I was prepared!

She asked, given that I had willingly and enthusiastically took the trips and time with the child and his mother, why did I suspect that the boy was not my son?

My reply centered around my and my attorney's legal strategies. Just like the opposing lawyer coached her client, my lawyer had coached me.

To save the court time and her effort, I cut her questioning short and immediately agreed that the child was my son and that we could move on to other areas of questioning.

I then countered, asking my questioner:

"Where is my boy?"

Well, he was the central focus of the proceedings, right?

Without answering my question, the lawyer pressed on, asking why I stopped paying child-support. "Didn't you think that the boy eats and needed clothing?" the lawyer insisted.

I again asked, "Where is my son?"

I was well prepared for this area of questioning. I knew that sooner or later it would be brought up.

I then presented the mound of my receipts for my payments and expenditures, thousands of dollars, sent to the mother for the child or used to buy needs for the mother and the child – all with no court order forcing me to do so and without a child to see and hold.

I answered her question, as to why I stop sending money. I said that I had not heard from or had learned nothing about the child for a long time. Calls went unanswered, emails never returned.

The courtroom discussion continued, and then the judge turned to the mother and requested the child's whereabouts. Almost instantly, the trial turned in my favor, shifting more toward my relationship with the child. One would expect the mother to be more favored in a woman-leaning court, but things were moving in the other direction.

The mother's lawyer, to disrupt the judge questioning her client, stood up in front of the judge and stated that her client had a lawyer – not a wise thing to tell a judge. The judge ordered the attorney to sit down and then he continued the cross examination.

"When you came to the U.S. for these proceedings," the judge said, "asking the court for monetary compensation, did you contact Mr. Cordero to tell him his son was coming?"

Her answer: "No."

The judge responded: "Why would you not answer emails or phone calls?"

The mother answered: "We were not on talking terms, your honor, and I was relying on my attorney's advice."

The judge pressed further: "Did you contact Mr. Cordero when you landed at the airport with his son?"

Her answer: "No."

"When you landed," the judge insisted, "did you tell the child that his father wasn't there to receive him because you didn't tell him?"

Again, she said: "No."

"When did you tell Mr. Cordero that his son was here in the U.S.?" the judge asked.

"A month later, your honor."

In frustration, the judge pounded on the podium, his voice booming throughout the courtroom: "May I ask, why on earth did you wait a month, after flying 18 hours from

Europe, to tell the father that his son was here or for the child to see his father?"

She said: "Well, my lawyer instructed me to avoid all contact with the father."

The judge went silent and stared at the attorney for a while, showing his displeasure. He requested to see all my receipts, and I happily handed them to him.

The mother's attorney continued cross-examining me; she walked to the judge and flipped through my receipts with the intent of discrediting me. This small woman came right up to me and pressed her face against mine, shouting, "You seem to have a temper, Mr. Cordero. You seem like an angry person."

I responded, informing her that she was too close to my face and that she had very bad breath.

She walked back to the judge's bench and continued examining my receipts. "There are only three receipts where you sent over a thousand dollars." I had not been under any legal obligation to send that much money.

I said: "If you were to find only one, it would still prove that I am telling the court the truth. One is all that's needed, but you found three." I had previously indicated that I had sent payments of up to $1,000 to the mother and child.

Concerning the more recent time when I sent no money, the lawyer proceeded to request that retroactive child-support be required of me for that time period. She requested that appropriate interest and penalties be enforced. Further, as I had previously corresponded with her office, even challenging her and the mother's allegations, the attorney requested that the judge order me to pay her legal expenses for additional research and time spent on my challenges.

She wanted what would have been a fortune to me, and in court you can ask but that does not mean you'll get.

I also produced and showed the judge several printed air-fare quotes from airlines and estimates of hotel-stay and meal costs for the costs that I would incur to fly to see my child. All of this information proved valuable for my case and assisted the judge in making decisions. The judge thanked me for the papers and cautiously reviewed them. The mother's lawyer stared from a distance.

Turning to the judge, I added: "If the mother and I were given 15 minutes by this court to be by ourselves, we could work out the differences and come up with an agreement satisfactory to both and to the court."

I continued: "The mother called me during her last visit and asked that I see the child. We took a trip together, and I even secured a passport for the child. We then sat down, your honor, and wrote down a very reasonable agreement, satisfactory to both. The agreement included a very generous amount of money for retroactive support. The mother was happy and I was happy. But then she contacted her lawyer to inform her of the agreement, and her lawyer talked her out of it. We are here today as the result of that action and are now adversaries."

The mother's attorney had no further questions for me.

I was still a bag of sweat, but things were not going in favor of this opposing lawyer; I was allowed to return to my seat.

Then my attorney's turn came to question the mother. She would sit on that gray chair and be crossed-examined.

My attorney took her time to approach the mother. Taking slow, short steps to the bench, this tall, imposing woman lawyer approached with an intimidating countenance on her face. I cannot fully describe how this almost giant of a woman appeared, looking down on my former lover.

"How much did you pay your lawyer?" my lawyer asked.

"$8,000."

"Where from did you get that kind of money?"

"I sold a land and also savings," the mother answered.

"How much did you sell it for?"

"84,000 Euros."

The judge interrupted and asked for the current Euro exchange rate to American dollars. I was the only person who, other than the mother, knew the conversion rate. I yelled across the room: "137,000 dollars, your honor."

My attorney seized an opportunity and requested that the mother write that amount in the paperwork submitted to the court. She had failed to do that when the documents were filed.

"That amount was not included in here," my lawyer insisted.

The mother at once wrote the inclusion.

But across the room, her lawyer griped as if with intestinal pain. Things were not going well for the top-dollar lawyer who had previously been heard to boast that she "would devour me in court."

I kept repeating silently to myself, "When you walk in righteousness, you leave footprints in the sand that neither wind nor time will ever erase. Let's win this."

My lawyer pressed the mother again: "The father should have had contact with your son, don't you think? At a minimum, hearing from him?"

She began to sob and nodded her head in agreement.

Both the judge and my lawyer asked the mother to ensure that I get to speak with the child when needed. They also mentioned that she should teach him English so he could understand and talk to the father and so he could boost his prospects of a better life and opportunities in the United States.

The mother became very cooperative and cordial with the court at this point. She even mentioned that, finances permitting, she would bring the child to spend time with the father in Texas.

"No, this is not a bad person," I thought to myself. "She is a good woman who conceived my most beautiful treasure. But just like me, she got caught up in the system and under the umbrella of a money-hungry lawyer."

The judge inquired about the child and his whereabouts, and I was able to receive the first valuable piece of information about him in many months. She said he was back home and under the care of his grandmother, well cared for.

"After the trial is done and lawyers are out of the way, make sure you bring him to see his father. Boys need their father," the judge added.

My attorney continued her courtroom work for me. A good portion of the trial was spent on cross-examinations and on revision of documents by both lawyers, lasting nearly 3 hours, and then both sides rested their cases.

Then something extraordinary happened yet again.

The judge concurred that this was a difficult case to decide as neither the mother nor the child resided in the United States. In a traditional woman-leaning court, as he moved forward to close **The Trial**, this judge handed me a silver tray -- a rare opportunity that, according to my lawyer, is unheard of in this type of case.

"If you were in my place, what would you decide?" the judge asked.

"Wow! It looks like I am winning this thing," I said to myself.

I said to the judge: "Your honor, given the record and the possibility that I might or might not see my child, the mother is not at fault but rather she is being well coached to deceive the court. I suggest that visitation take place in the U.S. where the court can see whether the order is obeyed or not. Further, I request that the child-support

188

money be deposited in an escrow and funds be disbursed according to adherence to the court order.

"In other words, no child, no money.

"I also respectfully request that I get a relief on the amount of child-support to be paid. There is a good chance that I will have to travel to Europe in order to spend time with my boy."

That was my answer and my plea.

I noticed the judge taking notes.

The Trial ended and the judge thanked everyone for her/his participation and then thanked the lawyers for their professionalism. I stood up, hugged my lawyer and walked out feeling fantastic.

Gloves off, fight over!

I just fought the law, I thought, and I took quite a few punches, but perhaps I won this battle!

Days later, I received a letter from my lawyer. A decision had been rendered by the court and before I opened the letter, I said a short prayer and asked God to help me accept whatever the judge decided — I was tired of fighting.

The judge wrote: "After considering both arguments by the participating lawyers and their clients, this court has reached a decision."

At last I will get to have some rights and a chance of a lasting relationship with my son, I hoped. In that earlier pre-trial appeal procedure, the short hearing that resulted in the senior judge declaring *The Trial* would deal with all the issues, he ordered the DNA tests. Results of the tests had shown that I was the father: "You are the father," the judge ruled. Johnny is carrying my DNA, according to all reasonable odds. The test results were declared to have 99.999999 percent accuracy.

The pre-trial test results led the judge to render another decision in **The Trial** and issue a court order. My lawyer sent me the letter. It read: "Results of DNA showed that father's paternity has been established. I therefore order that child-support in the amount of $500 be paid by the father each and every month."

This decision by the judge reduced the amount of child-support that I be required to pay to less than half what the rate would have been required under the Texas standard formula.

Call it a different name if you wish, but I think I won something here!

The judge added: "Visitation shall take place in the United States or any place the father chooses. Until the child is old enough, the mother shall purchase her own ticket and the child's ticket and bring him to the U.S. for the summer vacations and for every other Christmas. Father has a choice of visiting the child during spring break or any other time he chooses."

In yet another decision, the judge declared: "There will be no retroactive child-support paid by Mr. Cordero. Each litigant shall be responsible to pay his/her own attorney."

After the trial, as a result of this retroactive child-support decision, the mother's lawyer requested a hearing with the judge to discuss, you guessed it, retroactive child-support. It cost me additional attorney's fees to deal with that.

There are several extraordinary and exceptional victories here: First, I won my right to be a father and to be declared Johnny's dad. Second, against some tough odds, I located my boy in Europe, brought the case to a court in Texas and won it. *I fought this one and won it!* Unheard of in most cases, the judge reduced to less than half the usual child-support rate.

Additionally, as I requested during trial, visitations will take place at or near my home in Texas ... at the mother's expense.

The judge did come down on the mother and her lawyer and rendered a decision like no other. My child-support payments will, in large measure, go for travel expenses so my child can visit me.

Well, I mentioned that the word "fair" does not exist in the legal system; so, it works both ways. And this time, against a mother in a woman-leaning court. *A huge victory!*

On the bottom line, that mound of receipts won my case. And the judge dismissed more than $60,000 in potential retroactive child-support that I otherwise certainly stood to pay.

Almost everything the mother's lawyer requested was denied, and everything I requested was granted. That must be called what it is – I fought the law and won!

An unbearable load has been lifted off my back, the 900-pound gorilla was finally off me. I could finally rest and sleep in peace. My smile returned along with the desire to exercise. I began to lose weight and shape up and to socialize again.

In the months that followed I still pondered how I prevailed. I think that, in part, doing the right thing saved me. Credit those voluntary payments and those receipts, my trial/legal preparation, my experienced lawyer, a good and equitable judge, and being truthful to myself, the court and my lawyer. And certainly my deep desire to be with my boy kept me going.

All of those factors played a role in my success.

After all was said and done, the family court system and some of the judges sometimes have a heart, I said. I expected the worst, thought I would lose on every issue. Fortunately I reaped a very reasonable but rare judgment for an unwed father.

For most of you readers, sadly, it will not be this way!

For me, it was finally over ... or so I thought.

Chapter 9 – Just when I thought it was over … *The Appeal*

Unpleased with the results from the senior trial judge in Tarrant County's family court, the mother appealed.

I can only imagine what her attorney reasoned, and this was likely some of the advice given to the mother: The father wasn't satisfied with the results of the ruling from the associate judge; so he appealed and won with the senior judge. Now it's your turn. He has already been ordered to pay child-support; that's not going to change. You should appeal your case to the family court of appeals.

There were just a couple of little details that her attorney failed to mention: When you take your case to the appellate level of the court system, you pay . . . lots of money and you take on much higher risks. Typically, it's really more of an option for those folk well-heeled financially, who can afford to lose twice.

On my side, I was learning that appealing a case cannot be based simply on not liking the results. You must prove the original judge made errors in interpreting the law.

Family law judges have lots and lots of freedom, wide leeway, to decide the issues of almost any case. *It seems sometimes that they decide on a personal whim or wish!*

Therefore, DO NOT DECIDE to appeal an unfavorable judgment based on your emotions and frustrations. If you are swayed by your feelings, only, you could easily waste your time and money, and believe me, some lawyers will make you dream, take your money and file an appeal when the chances of winning are zero or nearly zero.

I believe there are plenty of wrong decisions by lower courts to be reversed.

Not too surprisingly, achieving justice becomes a problem, perhaps impossible, if you don't have sufficient money for an appeal.

If you are unable to appeal, if you don't have the money and energy, the original decision will stand. You lose. But I insist, while there are battles not worth fighting, there are others that are worth every ounce of fight that you can muster, and mine was one of these. You have to decide how your challenge rates, fight or not. If you fight, don't quit.

Unlike the losing outcomes of most other civil lawsuits, though, a loss on appeal in family court does not leave you the option of going the bankruptcy route to settle up. Rather, if you don't pay, you go to jail. It's the incarceration route! Child-support cannot be wiped out through bankruptcy proceedings – it will haunt you for a lifetime. Even in old age, it will be deducted from your Social Security or other retirement income before you ever get the deposit from Uncle Sam.

Filing an appeal becomes even less appealing when looking at the cost for something that's far less than a certain victory. Paying for an appeal of your case to be heard by a higher court, one attorney estimated, will likely start with a $10,000 retainer. Indeed, the legal appeals system is geared to the rich.

Return with me now to that thrilling moment when the associate judge ruled against me and wrote that the court had authority to order me to pay child-support but no authority to grant me access to my son.

I, accordingly, appealed that jurisdiction decision to the senior judge, which was not a full appeal to the court of appeals for family law cases. But when you challenge a family court ruling, you're also challenging the State of Texas, regardless of venue. In my case, I was challenging on a jurisdiction issue. My appeal, therefore, was sort of an informal, inexpensive and short hearing with both lawyers meeting before a senior judge in the same court. The hearing was a "Yes-or-No" matter, and the result was the decision for a full trial before the senior judge on jurisdiction and the other issues.

It may have been a short, informal hearing, but it was of major importance to me, and it was an official court hearing. So, when -- in this "yes-or-no" matter – the senior judge decided that establishing paternity was a top priority while also deciding the other major issues.

I had no doubts about being the father of the child involved in my case, But the judge wanted to know. So, in the short pre-trial hearing, he ordered the DNA testing even though I was not officially, legally, challenging my paternity.

Thereby, DNA tests were conducted on swabs of saliva taken from me, the mother and the child.

By itself, this path is not the costly option of filing a full appeal to a higher court.

However, for me it was inexpensive, nearly $400 combined total for all three tests. I thought it was going to cost more. You know, the prices on new technologies are coming down in many areas of science.

197

Contrary to the associate judge's opinion, the senior judge ruled a "Yes," the court had authority on all the major issues – jurisdiction, paternity and visitation and the child-support rate – because the Eastern European mother submitted herself and the child to the authority of the local court in Texas.

A full-blown trial on all the issues -- conducted before the same senior judge in the family court system – resulted from this quickie hearing and his rulings.

That trial, repeating, ended with me being the main winner without the child's mother suffering any major setback on child-support payments. That did not stop her from appealing, though.

In another important piece of this appeal puzzle, when you're aiming for the higher court of appeals, you've got to start with requesting a "reporter's record" from the trial court. These are the official transcripts and other typed notes taken during the procedures, motions, hearings and all earlier trials related to the same case. The records are not free of charge; currently, you spit out about $1,000 for them – assuming there was just one trial.

The scuttlebutt after the trial before the senior judge was gossip, but there had to be some serious grain of truth in this reasoning: "Don't be alarmed," her attorney was said to have assured the mother. "$1,000 is a lot of money. But we will win this appeal, and you will receive over $60,000 plus interest!" At the very least, her attorney must have advised the mother that she had a reasonable chance of prevailing in the court of appeals.

If so, and the reality certainly seemed to prove it, that lawyer was looking out for herself and her law firm's pocketbook.

Again, I emphasize, don't appeal a court decision based solely on your dissatisfaction or anger with the trial results. For an appeal to have merit, you must show that the lower court made legal errors in procedures or in applying the law in the decision-making process or that the judge made mistakes in interpreting the law. An appeal based solely on your displeasure over a decision or resulting solely from your anger against the judge, your opponent or otherwise probably has no merit and has no chance of prevailing.

In my legal proceedings, the mother was unhappy with the trial court decision, and that's an understatement. Thus, her attorney may have had little trouble convincing the mother to appeal. Sadly, the result was the mother appealing a verdict that proved to be "unappealable."

And thereby I received yet another letter from the court; it said in part: "Your lower court decision has been appealed." My translation: "Your victory might be temporary."

Everything I had accomplished, my savored victories in the trial, stood a chance to be reversed, I feared. Once again the monsters of doubt would come to haunt me, disturbing all ability to rest.

As I pondered yet another battle, with more money to be spent, I went outdoors to clear my head. In the summer months, the City of Fort Worth conducts a great number of outdoor music and family events. I decided to attend one of those events with friends, and ironically, I was introduced to the chief justice of the same appeals court handling the mother's appeal of my victory.

Man! I was excited to meet and chat with this celebrity.

I met the man who could help me, so I thought in my naïve legal way! We exchanged business cards. He was interested in inviting me to perform, sing, at the family law appeals court office Christmas party.

Days letter, I wrote the chief judge a letter explaining my situation and asking for his help. *What was I thinking!?*

Accordingly, his office responded to my letter: "We are in receipt of correspondence sent to the Chief Justice in connection to your case. ... Neither the judge nor the staff of this court can give legal advice."

That, of course, goes an infinite number of times more for any case coming before the appeals judges. You know, special treatment is cause for legal trouble for any judge giving it to a party in a case to be heard by the judge or his associates. The appeals court has three sitting justices on each appeal.

So, don't try anything like what I did; don't push it. Let the system run its course, and it's got to be impartial for justice to be served.

Did I sing at the family court of appeals' Christmas party? Of course not!

Know that, besides expensive, filing an appeal is complicated and requires superb technical legal knowledge. It is also very time consuming.

Here in this phase, I certainly could not represent myself, but then I had realized early on that I needed a good lawyer. This time I needed an appeals specialist.

Yes, as I've already said, I looked for and found the best appellate lawyer in the U.S. Southwest, another woman. That appellate star's fee rate sent me running out of the office quickly however.

I then located a younger but still bright lawyer and consulted him on a strategy to win the appeal. He was a laid-back sort of guy and talked as if we knew each other. He looked at my documents and saw the foolishness of the opposition in appealing and stated: "Judges in family courts have lots of leeway to decide and can decide any way they wish."

The same idea had been voiced by that brilliant and best of the Southwest appellate lawyer, the woman I had consulted but not hired, yes, the $10,000 attorney. She had read the appeals scripts and what the opposition was appealing and stated that judges have lots of discretion to make decisions. And appealing because the judge ordered the mother to pay for travel, she had said, is not winnable. The mother will lose, the lawyers agreed!

The lower fee-rate appellate lawyer I hired had a heart. He quoted me a discounted rate. Like a boxer, he said, his job would be to counter-punch with different citations and documentation than my trial lawyer used. He had to be able to refute all claims.

I didn't like it, but I was ready to put the gloves on again for another fight in court. In December 2008, my appellate lawyer notified the court that he was representing me in the case.

On February 24, 2009, the appellate fight began.

For the appeal, I was not required to be present. I chose not to be there. Neither was the mother. I opted to let the lawyers duke it out. I stayed out of my attorney's way.

The lawyers were scheduled first for oral arguments. In an appeal, there is no testimony from the parties to the lawsuit or from witnesses or experts in the case. Rather, the lawyers tangle with each other over legal issues, procedures or related case action at the lower court. The lawyers explain their positions, claims, arguments, and they answer questions from the three sitting judges.

The mother went from being the plaintiff to being the appellant. I went from being the defendant to appellee. But in court we were referred to by our first names.

Suddenly and unexpectedly, intriguingly, the mother's attorney did not show up for trial! Yes, this was a new appellate lawyer sent by the firm managed by the diminutive woman lawyer who had represented the mother at trial, then persuaded her to appeal and took her money. In other words, the mother's two attorneys – both women --

were employed at the same firm. I had relied on women serving as my attorneys until I reached the appellate level.

The new attorney was a no-show!

No explanations were ever given to the court for her absence. The court hearing however proceeded without her, and I got my information on the hearing later from court records, an audio recording of the hearing and my attorney's report.

My attorney – saying something like "may it please the court" – proceeded to present the arguments on both sides of the issues raised by the appeal. He presented documents and arguments for both sides. He was still my attorney of record, but he became something of a shadow lawyer, a courtroom shadow-boxer punching the air, working without a legal adversary to move the case forward in front of three judges. Why waste a day?

My attorney told the justices: "I have the enviable position of boxing against an adversary who is not in the ring with me. So, I better get in and dig out the facts."

Obviously, that's always good for you – when your lawyer shows up prepared and your adversary doesn't show up at all for this sort of pay-per-view event. I lost respect for that diminutive woman.

Let me make my position clear on this situation: The mother was lured into spending the money for an expensive appeal when she had zero chance of prevailing. Her new attorney, the woman knowing the situation, did not even appear to argue the case on the mother's behalf. This was a good example of taking the money and running! But again, I already warned you on chapter 4 about predatory lawyers. Indeed, strangely, the court took no action against this absentee lawyer.

Regardless, the court allowed my attorney to proceed with the arguments, punching air as the ghostly opponent and then punching for me. Fortunately for the appellant, the mother of my son, both lawyers had been required to submit written briefs before trial. The appeals court accepted the appellate lawyer's arguments in writing.

But I wondered at the time, privately: "How can a court give an appellant the same chance to win a case when that appellant's attorney doesn't even show up?" Indeed, the court took no action against this absentee lawyer, and the courtroom action began:

Argument #1 - from the appellant, via her attorney only in writing, voiced by my attorney: The senior trial judge abused his discretion in deviating from the state standard in assigning a child-support rate below the state standard. Texas, as most states, has its own guidelines on how to calculate child-support rates. The appellant argued that the judge erred in not providing justification for deviating and with that error made, the judge's order should be vacated, or dropped. If this had happened, the move would have provided the appellant an opportunity to take the case back to the trial court, perhaps with a different judge, and have a chance to win the case.

Counterpunching, refuting that argument, my attorney presented the court with a list of well-documented cases and rulings of trial courts in which trial judges opted to deviate from the state guidelines. My attorney argued:

"Family court judges have discretion to vary from the Texas statutory guidelines, upwards or downwards, based on relevant factors. These factors are known as 'the best interest of the child factors,' and the court's discretion in deviation from the statutory guidelines is allowed when considering the totality of the circumstances. Among these circumstances are:

- "... each party's period of possession of and access to the child;

- "...travel costs for exercising possession of and access to the child;"

My attorney further argued: "In Texas you don't abandon an order just because it's missing a few sentences, you abate it (fix it)."

In short, the senior trial judge had failed to write down why he adjusted the child-support rate by deviating from the state standard guidelines.

In the end, the appeals court ordered the trial court's oversight – failing to cite precedents for the deviation -- be corrected and sent the case back to the senior trial judge for that correction to be made by recording the stipulated reasons. The trial judge simply corrected the case paperwork by incorporating -- in his court order to me -- his legal reasoning for deviating from traditional rules.

That was the end of it – in the end, a waste of time and money!

Argument # 2 - centering around the senior trial court judge ordering the mother to spend child-support money for travel to meet the visitation requirements of the order:
The senior trial judge's order is unfair and burdensome to the mother and requires spending money otherwise needed

for the child's welfare. By doing this, the judge abused his discretion.

My attorney countered: "That's an argument that has no appeal merit as it is left to the discretion of the trial judge to order."

The senior trial judge had ruled that "until the child is old enough to travel without a parent, mother shall pay the cost of her ticket to travel with the child." To obey this part, the mother would have to purchase a $1,500 round-trip ticket for herself and another $850 for the child to fly to the United States, then pay for lodging for both, for local transportation and for food – for two summer months of visitation – before returning home to Eastern Europe.

My attorney said: "Endless court cases support the trial judge in this decision. She must bring the child to the U.S. at her expense because the trial judge uncovered ample reasons to believe his order was not going to be obeyed. After all, what power can the court exercise should this part of the order be disobeyed?"

Argument # 3 - centering around the senior trial judge deciding to reject payment of retroactive child-support – to be paid by me – : Retroactive child-support payments won't be a burden on Mr. Cordero because he already had offered the mother $12,000 in retroactive support prior to any legal action being taken. And, the argument continued, Mr. Cordero failed to pay any child-support for nearly five years.

My attorney responded: "I have presented to the court in writing scores of cases in which the court denied request for payment of retroactive child-support. In this case, the findings showed that the father might have to travel to Europe to visit the child. Further, he was denied his right to see his child or know his whereabouts."

NOTES: The mother, on advice from her attorney, rejected that $12,000 pre-litigation offer of mine. After sending monthly pre-litigation payments of $500 to $1,000 or more to the mother for five years, I halted my monthly payments. The halt continued for nearly five years because the mother kept me from seeing the child and kept me from knowing the child's whereabouts, health condition, education and all other pertinent child-rearing matters.

After an hour and a half of arguments and questions by the justices, my attorney rested my case. Later he shared with me that he felt good about the questions asked by the justices and the tones of their voices.

The court adjourned for the justices' deliberations. Then began our long wait.

Contrary to the trial court's more expedient action, the court of appeals may take six months or longer to make a decision.

The mother's appellate lawyer was never heard from, vocally in court, and she resigned from that law firm and seemed to disappear from the planet! My lawyer sent follow-up correspondence, but a different lawyer responded.

A couple of months passed until finally my appeals lawyer phoned me. With cold cruelty in the tone of his voice, he began walking me through a letter received from the court of appeals. He timed every word and inflection as if trying to inflict a deeper wound into my worried heart.

My lawyer read to me via the phone, from the appeals judges' verdict: "We would rule differently from the trial judge. . . . We concur that a different outcome and decisions could have been made."

I was in agony.

Then my attorney's tone changed and he broke the news:

"You won your appeal!"

He had been playing a bit of a nasty joke on me, at first, before sharing on the victory. *What a son of a biscuit eater!*

First, the court decided that only the stated reasoning was missing from the senior judge's court order, his reasoning for deviation from the state standard for calculating child-support rates. So, that was just a matter of rewriting the original order, while not changing the judge's decision.

On Argument #2, the appeals justices decided to sustain the trial senior judge's decision, confirming that he had that discretion based on circumstances of the specific case. Mother must pay for travel. There was no abuse of discretion by the trial judge.

On Argument #3, the justices sustained the trial senior judge's rejection of retroactive child-support payments. Again, the justices cited the discretionary authority of the trial judge. There was no abuse of discretion by the trial judge.

"This court finds that the trial judge did not overstep his authority," the justices wrote. "We find no errors in the administration of the law."

Finally, the justices declared: "The decisions of the trial court are sustained in their entirety."

Without any significant reservations, they sided with me. I was surprised, an understatement. More accurately stated: Flabbergasted!

Years later, today, I still feel exhilarated when I think of the fabulous news from the appeals court.

How did I defeat, twice, formidable adversaries – one so-called top-rung family lawyer and a second one who turned out to be a flop while failing to show for the appeals proceedings? These two women lost in a woman-leaning family court system. I still ponder this outcome. How did I convince 4 judges-a trial judge and 3 appellate justices, to side with me in all and every single aspect of the case?

I'm also still wondering: "Have I seen the end of this legal adventure? Did I get the absolute final word on all of this?"

I'm hoping and I do feel somewhat confident that I won't see any further challenges to the decisions handed down.

"An appeal could still be made to the Texas Supreme Court. However, I don't think the high court would consider something like this," my attorney assured me.

"As far as I am concerned, this is the end," my attorney said after the appellate results came in, back in 2009.

Years have gone by and I haven't been served with any new legal papers, and I have not heard from any lawyers or court clerks, so far.

Broken and bruised for many years afterward, but at peace!

Chapter 10 - *The Hall of Shame, notes on true deadbeats ...*

People are humorous sometimes when providing reasons and excuses for foolish acts. I found some of that humor, albeit on the bitter or dark side, during a random survey I conducted of deadbeat parents.

I approached a number of people whom I thought either knew someone with an unusual child-support/custody experience or had one of their own.

I visited a number of bars with a few friends and spoke to some of their acquaintances and others, dozens of people; I chose bars because, I'm convinced, drunks or otherwise frequent drinkers are often among the most generous givers of money and personal unsolicited information.

If you wish to know what is happening in the world or the neighborhood, go to a bar and listen; they'll tell you everything. Drunks know everything or think they do.

I asked one question to each of my interviewees: "Why won't you or why didn't you pay child-support?"

Here are some of the various answers I received. I give only first names, to protect the innocent and honor confidentiality that I promised for their comments.

Robert: "My ex was not going to use the money for the kid; so, as self-employed, I hid my money from the court. I paid very little."

Andres: "I quit my job on purpose so I didn't have to support her. She would use the money on dope and booze."

Joe: "I already had two other kids to support and, currently, another one on the way."

Michael: "I give my ex-wife plenty of money on the side. The state has no right to stick its nose in our personal lives."

Josh: "I never get to see my kid."

George: "She tricked me; she said she could have no more kids!"

Antonio: "I'll go to jail but she is not getting my money."

John: "Man, I requested child-support modification and was denied, after spending $2,000 in attorneys' fees and court costs. The hell with it!"

Anthony C: "Dude, I am an alcoholic and am on dope. I can't take care of myself much less support a kid."

Dean: "I asked her to get an abortion but she refused."

Ralph: "She doesn't need my money. She makes twice what I make."

Carlos: "I owe so much back child-support that I'll never catch up."

Cesar: "My employer failed to take it out of my paychecks and I now owe retroactive plus interest and penalties."

Marcus: "I already went to jail once for it. I don't think it is going to fix anything."

William: "I gave her the house and money; that's enough."

Gabriel: "She cheated on me, and now I am expected to support her and the new man, who sleeps in my house where my kids live?"

David: "I am 67 years old…they can get it from my social security check, when I get one."

"Junior" (The man who would not give his real name): "I don't believe I owe it! She is gone, I am gone…we good."

Ed: "She receives three checks for $1,200 a month for the three summer months, another one for Christmas, and one more for Spring Break when the kids are with me. The court does not give me any credit for that! I am now unemployed and must go to court, hire a lawyer, to change the amount. The hell with it!"

And here is the first-prize explanation/excuse of all, among those I heard, for not paying child-support:

Arthur: "I was in a car wreck a few years back, died and had to be resuscitated. Child-support ceases when you die, doesn't it? That's why I don't pay."

(NOTE: All of the above explanations/excuses for not paying child-support are based on purportedly real stories of and by deadbeats – or so they said.)

I never wanted to be a deadbeat dad, and never was, but I sort of had a logical excuse for delaying or temporarily halting my child-support payments. Here's the situation I faced:

After the final verdict in my case, it was time for both of us to abide by the judge's orders.

For my first visitation, the mother brought Johnny to the United States as ordered.

A few days later, however, she took the child away.

I called her and asked about my son and his whereabouts; she stated she had him and would tell me in a while where he was, so I could pick him up.

I did not hear from her until midnight and informed her I would be coming by to pick up my son. She stated that she would text me the address so I could get him. She texted me the address to pick up my son next morning before I headed to work, but – I thought, maliciously -- the address was a 3-and-a-half-hour drive away from my house! I, of course, needed to be at work!

She had just violated the court order. A battle began again!

I told her that I would not be picking the child up but would contact the court and let them deal with her.

Next morning, my lawyer called after being contacted directly by the mother. The lawyer informed me that I needed to work things out with the recalcitrant mother.

I was advised that the court cannot fix everything.

The best that could be done was for her to be required to appear in court with the child and be reminded of her obligations.

But, given that the mother had only a few more days in the United States, that approach was not practical!

In essence, the woman could violate the prohibition of interference in my access/visitation rights, and it could be difficult or impossible to rectify the situation. But just try to violate the adjudicated payment of child-support and see what happens!

That thought had crossed my mind, as retribution for her preventing me from visiting my son.

If you don't pay as the judge says, her attorney will have you put you in jail. For her, the worst that might happen for her violation, according to my counsel, was to be fined.

The mother was reluctant about bringing the child for my visit. For my part, her situation was a matter for the court to reconsider, if the judge agreed to it.

My attorney advised that I offer to pay all travel expenses and hotel for her to come and stay in Texas for my visitation; he said this was the best option if I expected to see my child, and then my attorney would ask the judge to order her to reimburse me the money.

I followed his recommendation. I incurred, in addition to child- support, an additional $2,800.00 in plane tickets for both, mother and child, their meals and their hotel stay.

A few days later my attorney went to court to petition that I be reimbursed.

The judge granted my petition, and the mother was ordered to reimburse me via my attorney's office. He called me to give me the "good news" that the judge signed the order for reimbursement, *but he added that it was NOT worth the piece of paper it was written on!*

The mother never obeyed the order, never paid, and the court took no action against her!

Well, she resides in a foreign country, away from the court's jurisdiction. If I decided to withhold child-support, though, I would end up in jail.

That's called justice!

And that's why I briefly considered becoming a deadbeat dad.

But I never took that step. I wanted my son to have the best possible life I can help deliver! I try to look for pragmatic, considerate, cooperative, compromise and/or reasonable solutions when conflicts arise in the ongoing relationship I have with my former lover.

Chapter 11 – *Courtroom behavior and ethics ...*

If you, regrettably, end up in court, you'll need some pointers on how to make a positive impression and, hopefully, give a boost to your case.

We've discussed the legal world of parental responsibilities. Yes, sure, it's critical to learn all you can about the commonly held views on those responsibilities and about family law pertaining to child custody/visitation, child-support, attorney, jurisdiction and paternity issues. So, go learn ... in advance of any legal action. But there's more to this prep.

Now it's time to get down to the essentials!

I received good advice from a few of my lawyers and from others on proper courtroom behavior and ethics. I've also come up with a few of my own tips to help you impress the judge and the court as a whole.

Court/courtroom etiquette, for a favorable impression – never underestimate the importance of image.

Maybe you don't have to impress the judge and lawyers, including your own, with a favorable image to receive fairness and a reasonable judgment and hopefully, justice. Maybe you should. ***You SHOULD!***

Regardless, at a minimum when trying to win in court, *ya gotta **NOT** look or act or talk like a fool, deadbeat, bum, spiteful spouse, cold-hearted bastard or selfish bitch!*

Do not forget the simple behaviors that work in most of our world at large: Yes, use the words, "thank you" and "please" and "may I." They work surprisingly well in making a good impression and sometimes reap miracles, getting people to listen to you. If you don't have those manners, adopt them before your case is heard. Too many people today have never been taught manners, by parents or anyone.

Here are some additional pointers born out my experience and research that will help you in court:

1. Dress in casual but still court-appropriate attire.

Think *"going to church":* Wear pressed or unwrinkled slacks and shirt, maybe a tie and near office-type coat/jacket, all in conservative colors – dark for slacks and coat, white or blue or muted green or stripes for the shirt – with nothing distracting on the tie and little or no jewelry showing anywhere. That means nothing in your nose, ear (except unpretentious earrings for women), tongue, lip, eyebrow, other facial feature or other visible site.

Attire should yell neither "I'm wealthy" nor "I'm poor." And overdressing, as for walking down the red carpet for the Oscars, will almost certainly make you a loser. The opposing lawyer will feast on that.

For women, don't try to be sexy or rebellious; going bra-less isn't wise. Revealing cleavage is probably a bad idea. **Think "my *granny is watching.*"**

Yes, wear socks or hose, dark or muted colors only. Do NOT wear tennis shoes, flip-flops or beach shoes. Sporting raggedy or holey jeans, mini-skirts or shorts is unwise. Wearing them low on your butt or hip would be stupid. Make sure you're wearing underwear, but not revealing it anywhere.

The courtroom is not a place to show how "cool" you are.

2. You want to smell good.

But strong perfumes are self-defeating. Either you're trying to hide your poor hygiene or you're aiming for sexual attraction. Neither works for you in court. **Think "I'm not going out on a date."**

Years ago, I recall, when going out on a date, I was unable to get close to the girl — her strong perfume being so irritating. I had trouble breathing. I actually asked her to wash some of it off.

Do not show up for court smelling like Scarlett O'Hara trying to finagle cash out of Rhett Butler or like the nectar of the gods, a keg room of Jack Daniels distillery or the barley-hops-rye of the tavern!

The judge, attorneys, court reporter and the rest will not think well of you or your manners if your hygiene is slack, lacking or overbearing or your tippling is out of control.

3. Beware of halitosis. *Bad breath!*

Brush your teeth thoroughly at home; use mouthwash.

Then have mints handy for the hearing; in court, do NOT chew gum.

Don't get too close to the judge if you have bad breath. He or she just might send you out to brush your teeth or gargle with Listerine.

4. Show respect at all times for the court and its officers, especially the judge and all lawyers.

That goes without saying, of course.

But ya gotta remember that your emotions may run high during the hearing, and you need to hold them in check most of the time. If you absolutely disagree with something said or your opponent says something that is accusatory of you and/or untruthful, you will get your chance to state your side of the story or issue.

And never call anyone "dude" in court.

Everyone is expected to acknowledge the presence of the judge or magistrate. When the judge enters or leaves the courtroom, you stand up. Just like in the movies or on TV – even if you have never done it for anyone and you have the "*I stand up for nobody*" attitude, do it this time.

6. Always be courteous to your adversary – your current or former spouse or spouses and her attorney/their attorneys.

Don't love! Don't hate! You are there to win this one.

7. Be on time for all hearings, especially trials.

Judges have often dismissed cases or ruled favorably for one party when the other party or his/her attorney is late. Lawyers are commonly reprimanded for arriving late. You already have enough barriers/hurdles/challenges to overcome; don't aggravate the judge or lawyers.

8. Turn off your cell phone before entering the courtroom.

Most courts now have a "No Cell Phone Allowed" sign displayed on the door. If your cell phone chimes, sings, rings, burps or dings during proceedings, a judge just might confiscate your phone.

I was in court a few years back assisting a friend when suddenly, a cell phone went off in the middle of proceedings. The judge immediately instructed the bailiff to confiscate it.

9. In the courtroom, sit in a manner which minimizes disruption.

That means sitting up, not reclining or sprawling, not eating in the courtroom and not talking to yourself or the person next to you.

Listen quietly.

10. Speak only when you're asked to speak by the judge or the lawyers.

Be courteous, try not to argue about anything, and be positive, upbeat, optimistic.

Don't address the opposing lawyer unless you are asked to do so. When asked to speak, talk – *do not yell!* You don't want to appear to be combative, disrespectful, anxious, nervous, angry or hostile.

11. Let your attorney be your lawyer.

I emphasize: Try to talk ONLY to your attorney. What sounds or seems appropriate to you might not be allowed in a court of law. Your attorney should coach you on these matters well before going to court. He or she should know how to present your arguments.

If you cannot follow these simple tips, maybe you need another lawyer.

12. Work/cooperate/prepare with your attorney; follow his/her directives.

Provide as much assistance as possible. For example, I was asked about airfare prices on roundtrips from/to Eastern Europe and Dallas, Texas. I immediately provided a copy of expenses for my last flight. Documentation is better.

Don't offer "I think it's something like . . ."

Being prepared for your court appearance is obviously important. But many litigants are not; the proof has been common in the courtrooms of the world.

Prep yourself on the basics of court procedure.

Understand that family court judges have wide and deep leeway to make decisions, all within the content/context/parameters of the law. You don't want to lose your case over foolishness; you're spending lots of your money.

227

13. Open carry – think: *"Am I stupid; do I really think the judge will like my handgun?"*

Going armed doesn't bode well for you in court. Leave your pocket knife at home. Bring nothing that could be construed as a weapon.

Courts have installed metal detectors for all individuals entering, and guards, screening machines, metal detectors and bag checks are common. You will be required to empty your pockets, and bags will be scanned.

14. Go to the restroom before stepping into court; you are expected to be there physically at all times during the session.

Coming and going will be disruptive, disrespectful and counterproductive – in the courtroom. Ensure that you don't airbrush your boxers! Don't flatulate; don't pass gas in court. Don't belch.

You will probably get a bit bored, but the court is not an entertainment center. You had the choice to avoid all of this, but didn't make that choice.

15. I know the issues are likely swirling around a child or children. But, unless the judge or lawyers request or recommend the little one's/ones' presence, leave the child/children at home with a reliable sitter.

Now you're ready to go in there, tell the judge the truth, support your attorney's efforts to win fairness from the judge, and if you don't succeed, appeal your case.

Chapter 12 – *Murky clouds in the system*

My adventure led me to be convinced that many improvements are needed for our family law system pertaining to child-support, visitation and related matters. My view is supported by Arlyn Villegas, an author on the subject and a senior social worker who has worked for 20 years on the Supreme Court with families, in the family court system. In her words: "It is a bureaucratic and sometimes unjust system."

Here are some but not all possibilities for improvement, and I call them "murky clouds" because more understanding of the law is needed and perhaps someone has better ideas than I do:

Murky cloud 1: A woman may be ordered by the court to reimburse the man for additional expenses he incurred; she may fail to do so with no consequences.

In my case, that judge's order wasn't worth the paper it was written on. The mother lives overseas; there's no one who can ensure she complies with the order; in fact, she probably cannot be served with the order. So, I lost more than $2,000.00.

Reasonably, the mother hired a lawyer, her lawyer was present when the order was signed, and her lawyer acting as "power of attorney" could relate the message to the mother and ensure the order be followed. Yes, the same lawyer who went after me ferociously, the one who insisted on enforcing the law and righteousness, chose to do nothing of the kind!

This lack of enforcement being applied both ways is a huge flaw in the system.

Murky cloud 2: Any child custody/support order contains a clause wherein it states that child-support ceases once the child completes high school, among other requirements.

In my case, my very bright son may finish high school at an age earlier than 18. If that happens, there will be no relief on paying child-support. The mother will likely not appear in court for a hearing. The law does require that she be informed, served with a notice of hearing, but she is not in the United States. I will be obligated to continue child-support payments even though my son finishes high school at 15 or 16. I believe that will happen.

231

I might be able to petition the court (thereby spending more money) to order an end to my obligation to pay child-support. But to do so, the court system requires that the custodial parent be notified of the petition and hearing and that proof of graduation be presented. In my case, the hearing and termination may not happen.

Murky cloud 3: A significant flaw in the system -- the parent who pays child-support cannot deduct the amount from his/her taxable income, or otherwise use that amount to reduce his/her taxes.

The Internal Revenue Service rules do not allow it. That's actual money, well documented spending, hopefully used by the custodial parent to benefit the child. Although it's not income available for any other purpose, it's taxable as ordinary income, taxable on the non-custodial parent making the payments, not on the custodial parent benefiting from the help.

The child being supported is not considered a dependent for the non-custodial parent, but is considered a dependent for the custodial parent receiving the money.

In short, the taxpaying non-custodial parent is being punished for having to pay child-support. Meanwhile, the custodial parent reaps the paid support and the deduction for the dependent child.

Murky cloud 4: Another significant flaw relates to additional child-support payments made.

The system does a good job of tracking regularly scheduled, court-ordered payments and crediting that child-support when paid. But additional payments can fall through the cracks as "gifts." Such payments are not credited.

Child-support will only cease for the following reasons: death of the child, upon his/her 18 birthday or high school graduation, the child's marriage, the child's entry into military service or the child's otherwise emancipation from his/her parents/guardians, or the court's termination of payments due to the paying parent's mental and/or medical/physical condition, disabilities or maybe other factors.

To terminate child-support, the payer must petition the court and convince the court that he/she has fulfilled his/her court-mandated obligations, or that he/she has paid the total amount required under the court orders, or that he/she cannot fulfill the obligations for whatever reasons. Getting a hearing on the petition can take months, and justifying the reasons can be a difficult, often impossible challenge.

And while credit generally is given for paying court-mandated monthly rates in advance, credit may not be granted automatically for overpayments. Typically there is no set, total, final amount or goal designated for payment.

But wait, if you are responsible enough and make additional payments beyond the order to pay off early, the system might step in and even consider raising your child-support rate; it will be assumed that you have more money and can afford to pay a higher rate.

Murky cloud 5: No deductions, reductions or credits are granted whenever the child spends summer months with the non-custodial parent.

The custodial parent still receives the full child-support amount even though that parent will normally have few or no expenses related to the child during the away time.

On several occasions, custodial parents have taken child-support windfall money and gone on vacations or made down payments on large purchases such as new cars. One can imagine a non-custodial parent receiving $800.00

a month in child-support for three summer months --
$2,400.00. Add whatever savings the non-custodial reaps
while the child is away for three months living with the
non-custodial parent. Then you can see that the summer
income boost might be tempting for one's own use, not the
child's.

The system lacks a mechanism to credit the non-
custodial parent for additional expenses incurred during
summer visits.

Murky cloud 6: In the event that a custodial parent gives
up the child to the state for care and hopefully for adoption,
the law stipulates that the former custodial parent and the
non-custodial parent now must pay child-support to the
state.

Murky cloud 7: The incarceration route for non-payment
of child-support must be revised so as not to be the only
final option.

Many people suffer emotional, mental, physical
and/or other psychological and medical conditions which
they cannot manage. The outcome can be a futile
imposition of child-support requirements on someone who
cannot care for himself/herself. How can you require a

demented, psychotic, neurotic and/or crippled or physically disabled parent to care for a child, particularly at support rates that were applied to an able-bodied, mentally normal parent capable of working and earning a livelihood?

Prisons hold too many of these dysfunctional parents failing to pay court-ordered child-support rates. And while the non-custodial parent remains in prison, child-support obligations still accumulate.

Murky cloud 8: Often a non-custodial parent (the one paying child-support) earns less money than the custodial parent but still must pay the same child-support rate set prior to the custodial parent's upswing in income. And there is the frequent situation that develops wherein the custodial parent remarries, and the new spouse earns more than the non-custodial parent.

In a particular case I mentioned earlier, a man pays a child-support rate that was based on his ex-wife being unemployed. He still must pay that rate although the ex has remarried, this time to a very wealthy businessman with an income fifteen times more than her former husband.

As much as possible or reasonable, child-support rates should be set in such manner as to allow both parents to live decent and comfortable lives – that is, child-support should the responsibility of both parents, not just the non-custodial.

Imagine a non-custodial father taking his children for a weekend visit, and they have to reside in a 1980 Pontiac – the only home he can afford after paying child-support and his other bills. Similar situations are too common in Texas.

Does that reflect "the best interest of the child"?

As I wrote these lines while savoring a cup of coffee in my favorite French Café, an acquaintance came by and asked about my writing. I then shared a summary of my book.

He then proceeded to tell me the true story of a woman, formerly married to his cousin, who stood in line at a casino holding a child-support check in her hand. She bragged about having plenty of money and that "this is play money," meaning the father's child-support payments to her.

Little did she know that the rules of life occasionally play you when you think you are playing them. Right behind the woman stood a close friend of the father who wrote the "play money" check for his kid's child-support.

While the father struggled to support his kids via a basic salary, she bragged about using the money as play money. Accountability must also be applied to the recipient of the money. I dare say, that father took action against his ex, hopefully in court.

Murky cloud 9: While in prison for cases unrelated to child-support, prisoners are still required to pay child-support as determined by family courts.

My opinion is: this situation was developed primarily for cases where the criminal hides money instead of paying child-support. The deadbeat parent has the means to pay, can pay -- but doesn't. For the majority of prisoners, however, it is a burden that they must carry for a lifetime.

Too often this kind of support case hits impoverished parents with few skills to earn a decent livelihood, and it tends to perpetuate poverty while not delivering much help to the children.

As the first black commander and chief of a nation that incarcerates a disproportionately large number of black and Latino men, President Obama made it a priority to address problems that make it difficult to impossible for released inmates to successfully re-enter society. The new rules require that prisoners be allowed to lower the amount of child-support they pay while they're in prison, with the goal of preventing large debts that inmates struggle and often fail to repay after release – a situation that can lead to reincarceration.

Murky cloud 10: A woman from any country may, at any time, and without setting foot in the United States, sue a man and petition a court to grant her child-support, and too often, without research or investigation, the court will oblige.

However, in the event the woman chooses to never send the child for visitation, as ordered by the court, at most, she would simply be penalized with a small fee. This penalty, of course, must be sought by petition filed by the non-custodial parent at his expense; otherwise, nothing would happen, no justice would be forthcoming.

One can imagine what would happen if the child died, if the child is given away for adoption, or is simply abandoned.

As she is no longer under this country's legal jurisdiction territory, she would continue receiving the child-support!

Enforcement should cover all areas, not just monetary.

When the custodial parent, almost always a woman, decides to deny visitation and violates a court order, seldom are there consequences.

Murky cloud 11: There are reciprocal family law agreements between/among countries that are wonderful at protecting children.

However, the "reciprocal country" in some cases does not live up to the agreement.

Consequently, the American father can be stuck with a court order that goes one-way, and his parental rights are not respected. He can do little or nothing!

The court will usually say, "We can do nothing about the mother violating the order as she is not here, but we have you."

This must change. The system must be equitable, meaning that they be enforced similarly by/in both/all pertinent countries. Both parents must be held accountable.

A boy needs his father and his mother, and that right of the father must be protected in a system that has been heavily weighted for the mother.

Murky cloud 12: The family law system must also provide better legal assistance for those unable to pay, as to prevent a parent heading to certain financial catastrophe.

A court should not exist for the purpose of ruining a man's life, both financially and reputationally.

The system still seems designed to ruin a man and enrich lawyers. In the end, the court must serve parents and children, and no one is served by ruining the father's capability of living and earning sufficient income to support the child.

Murky cloudy 13: In the event that the child grows wealthy, and does not need financial support from either parent, in today's system child-support is still ordered and its collection is enforced.

Will the child be ordered to pay support to the poorer parent or parents?

Parental support, if the child is that successful, why not?

Murky cloudy 14: In some states, child-support continues for adult children as long as they are in school or as long as they are legally, physically or mentally disabled

That schooling after high school typically means pursuing masters and/or even a doctorate degree or a technical/job degree/certification or license, continuing all the way to the age of 25.

I know some parents who pay child-support for adult children as they continue in school. This can serve to push a parent to poverty in old age. Then the government and taxpayers will become the caretaker for the impoverished elder parent.

Murky cloud 15: Often, men are incarcerated based on a warrant signed by a magistrate who has little knowledge of facts. Magistrate judges oftentimes are not lawyers who are familiar with criminal proceedings. As such, a magistrate cannot sign off on a bond for a class-A felony charge, but they can sign-off on the arrest warrant for a class-A felony charge. The system needs reforming that would require the signature of an actual prosecutor or criminal court judge on arrest warrants for felony charges. Many abuses of the system can be curtailed.

Murky cloud 16: Adjustments should be made on the child-support rate paid to a woman in a foreign country to reflect reasonable amounts for a livelihood for both parents, so as not to enrich or impoverish either party.

If the non-custodial parent lives on a middle-class income, the same should apply to the recipient of child-support. Equity for the parents will benefit the child.

Murky cloud 17: Plainly stated, how can a civilized society incarcerate a man for owing $1,000? On the other hand, countless individuals who rack up debt into the millions are allowed to wipe out that debt through bankruptcy! Often, multiple times; ask our President Donald Trump. Child support debt supersedes any other debt but, incarcerate someone for a $1,000 debt constitutes "cruel and unusual punishment. Won't it be?

In conclusion, a system is in place to care for children who would otherwise be destitute. However, significant changes are needed to avoid unjust incarceration and devastation of otherwise honorable men.

Conclusions

Family courts exist for good reasons. In spite of the legal system's flaws, I was impressed by the many tools available to assist parents ordered to pay child-support, and I came out victorious on all major aspects of my case, even the $500 monthly support rate that I was ordered to pay. I wanted to do it.

The Office of the Texas Attorney General's Child Support Division offers a variety of resources to assist when one has a problem. But it's far from perfect.

Although legal options and procedures have improved some, the changes have not been because the authorities and the voters have had pity or empathy for the little guys like you and me. We are of little value! Rather, lawyers, judges, senators and other influential people went through divorces and child-support cases; they've had a taste of what the system is like. *They wanted the changes and have worked to improve the system, Lord bless them!*

I understand that, yes, the system typically deals with repeat losers and deadbeats. On a visit to the child-support office in the beginning of my relationship with the system, for example, I saw a couple requesting to terminate

244

child-support. I noticed that the woman was nervous, scared, being coerced and almost threatened by the man as, after all, child-support is a debt to her. It was he who wanted to terminate child-support. When they left the office, I saw the man driving away in a brand new Mercedes-Benz!

For men like this, I am glad we have the system. Such deadbeats should be chased to the grave.

However, the system is just flat wrong, unfair, unjust in scapegoating men – singling out men -- for punishment, dooming them to a fate for a lifetime just because they're ignorant of the law and signed a piece of paper or were erroneously served legal papers. The system should move away from the business of ruining honorable, good men who simply cannot pay or who were not at fault for failing to meet their legal obligations.

Many otherwise good parents simply will never be able to pay. They may be too poor and so deep in debt they'll never climb to a level of income to meet their obligations. They may be incapable of earning a sufficient livelihood to meet those payment levels. Chronically indigent, uneducated, untrained, unskilled, emotionally unstable and demented parents just cannot live up to expectations.

Yet, they're too often chased to the grave for child-support payments that will never be made. Incarceration should not be the only alternative for deadbeat parents.

In many if not most of these cases, the system makes it impossible for them to have a fresh start; it becomes a life sentence.

Instead, devote more resources to go after the real criminals, the ones who can pay but purposely choose not to pay, regardless. They system already aims for these deadbeats, but it could do better.

The non-custodial parent should also be held more accountable, and not just for the monetary support/responsibility but also for visitation, actually parenting the child, helping to teach and guide that child.

The law needs to move away from the sole purpose of collecting money and toward paying more attention to the relationships between the parties and the rights of parents to be parents.

If the relationship is working out for both parents and the child/children, the best way possible, the state should stay out of the relationship. Why should the state intervene in a child-support case where the parties are happy and, then years later, step in to raise the amount of child-support as if to punish the payer? If child-support, as commonly and legally stated, is a debt to the mother, let the mother request such reviews, not the state. The impression is that the state intervenes for the sole purpose of collecting more money, just to show great numbers, so-called great enforcement results.

If it ain't broke, don't try to fix it.

Consequently, if the state continues its current practice of chasing evaders to the grave, the state will in the end be forced to care for a generation of elders who have been financially ruined. Who loses here?

Further, when a custodial parent lives in luxury and the other party visits the children while living in an old car or cheap motel, does this reflect the best interest of the child? Often, the non-custodial parent needs to work several jobs in order to provide for himself as well as the child/children. That is not a good system. A better system would consider the income of both parents. That approach is already practiced in some states.

Some parents have fought the same kind of battle that I did, but coming out with a different, less favorable outcome. That's tough. Like me, they have exhausted their finances and sacrificed much emotionally. For you folk, I wish my book had been there for you during your journey.

247

Now you can help someone like us; pass this book along and let them read it.

I like the pertinent advice of Holocaust survivor and psychiatrist Viktor Frankl: "If it is not in your hands to change a situation that produces pain, you can always choose the attitude with which to confront it."

Mine was a long, tiring, emotional journey; I wish this on no one. As in most serious battles of all types, the emotional scars can go on forever. I feel like an old lion weary of fighting, proud of my scars and looking for respite. I don't have much fight left in me; I hope it's over. I am constantly wondering, at any given time, if I will be receiving another letter from the court — one more time! I fear the possibility of some clerk of the court making a mistake that will cost me. An error that will exhaust the little money I have saved to, perhaps someday, if possible, retire honorably.

Yes, I will not be surprised to hear from someone in the legal system, trying to grab some share of the proceeds from the sale of this book, to give to the mother of my son.

I have prepared for this accordingly and will not profit from the sale. All proceeds from this book, after expenses, will be set up in an education fund for my son's future.

The mother, on the other hand, can earn as much income as she wishes or is able to earn, she can write and sell as many books as possible, and she will not be held accountable for sharing that income with our son. The system will cause no consequences to fall on her. *The system at times is not equitable. And dare I say, it's often not fair.*

Still with my journey, I fought The Law, and I won!

At the end, or the supposed end, I won but I also lost!

Yes, there was a decree from a court that was favorable to me. But I lost emotionally and financially ... precious time, 5,000 hours of research ... time that will never come back.

Additionally, I hope this book will help change the negative perceptions too many people hold about those lawyers, judges, law enforcers and others who, through the system, try to protect the interests of children.

Therefore, I no longer see the court as an adversary. I received a very fair, reasonable judgment, in a woman-leaning court.

I no longer see my son's mother as an adversary. I must give her credit for coming to terms with decisions that bring more benefits to our son and his future. After a tough battle, and thanks to her, I now get to be with him. She melted my heart with Johnny's first visit, when she said: "What a great father you are! You have become his hero."

I think however that my case was a worthy cause.

And now, after a few years have passed and the lawyers are out of the way, we -- Johnny, his Mommy and I -- are happy. I get time with Johnny any time I wish, and as he enters adolescence, he has even expressed his desire to move in with me. As I see him grow and show his brightness in school, he makes me proud; he's a kind, respectful, well-mannered young man!

I must add that the intent of this book is not to discredit the mother of my child; she is a good woman. Most of her actions resulted from her attorneys' advice and a system that allows lawyers to give misleading advice, and allows lawyers and clients to make errors that hurt children.

The mother is a special woman who gave me a son.

I appreciate that she drove my son to the airport in her hometown and allowed her little boy, her treasure, to board the plane alone and fly 5,635 miles away to spend the next two and half months with me. It was her desire for that experience to happen. Living in a distant land, she could disallow the visit if she wishes. After all, she has been his custodial caregiver, keeper; he is her life, her all!

I'm convinced that she sat in her car and watched that plane take off while she sobbed, praying that all would go well on the trip. She came to understand and accept that Johnny loves me, his Daddy, and that she could not stand in the way of something that means so much to him.

Johnny, this little boy, now speaks several languages, is at the top of his class, and has started a video games leasing company at the tender age of 13, his own "corporation" as he calls it. He has hired two classmates to assist.

Every single kid out there deserves what Johnny got . . . to be with his/her Dad, to spend time and have a real relationship with his/her hero.

While many parents have said goodbye forever, I can now say, "Welcome home, my little boy!"

Johnny makes my life worth living; I fought for him. Because of that, I am very rich! It was a fight for a worthy cause.

May this book bring you peace…

In pace re quiescat!

About The Author

Born in the public housing poverty of Puerto Rico, Johnny Cordero flunked out of school but came to cherish learning, eventually graduating from 3 American Universities and receiving a doctorate *Honoris Causa*. While growing up around drug addicts and criminals and muscling up to be a Golden Gloves boxer, he devoured cast-off books and was inspired by his self-sacrificing mother to create his own renaissance. Mr. Cordero drove himself to become an operatic tenor, song composer, actor, environmental specialist, and entrepreneur. His song *Mundo en Silencio* has won multiple awards; he has acted in theatre, television and had his own radio show at the tender age of 12. More recently he founded an alternative high school, and invented and holds a patent for the My Wearable Gym device. Now he has completed a book, *I Fought the Law ... and I Won!* about how he scrambled to be a good international father, relying on the same gutsy grit that drove his career successes.

By Journalist Worth Wren